FOCUS ON THE ®

the power of teachable moments

using everyday experiences to teach your child about God

jim **weidmann** &
marianne **hering**

Tyndale House Publishers, Inc.
Wheaton, Illinois

The Power of Teachable Moments

A Focus on the Family book
published by Tyndale House Publishers, Wheaton, Illinois 60189

Focus on the Family books are available at special quantity discounts when purchased in bulk by corporations, organizations, churches, or groups. Special imprints, messages, and excerpts can be produced to meet your needs. For more information, contact: Focus on the Family Sales Department, Focus on the Family, 8605 Explorer Drive, Colorado Springs, CO 80920; or phone (800) 932-9123.

Library of Congress Cataloging-in-Publication Data
Weidmann, Jim.
The power of teachable moments / Jim Weidmann, Marianne Hering.— 1st ed.
p. cm.
Includes bibliographical references.
ISBN 1-58997-120-5
1. Christian education of children. 2. Parenting—Religious aspects—Christianity.
I. Hering, Marianne. II. Title.
BV1475.3.W45 2004
248.8'45—dc22

2003021558

Editor: Tom Neven
Cover Design: Kurt Birky
Cover Photo: Mark Waters

Printed in the United States of America.
1 2 3 4 5 6 7 8 9 / 10 09 08 07 06 05 04

To Janet, the love of my life, whom I cherish very much.
Thanks for always being there to capture the "moments" in life for
our children and for impressing God's truths into their hearts.
Joshua, Jacob, Janae, and Joy call you blessed!

—J.W.

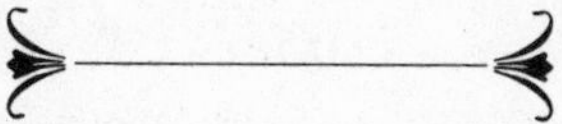

To those who live, laugh, and love with me—
Doug, Danielle, Justin, and Kendrick

—mkh

Table of Contents

Acknowledgments vii
Introduction 1

CHAPTER ONE
What Is a Teachable Moment? 5

CHAPTER TWO
Being Available—A Matter of Priorities 11

CHAPTER THREE
Parenting with a Purpose 33

CHAPTER FOUR
How to Teach Without Preaching 49

CHAPTER FIVE
A Good Relationship: The First Component of a Teachable Moment 73

CHAPTER SIX
The Catalyst: The Second Component of a Teachable Moment 101

CHAPTER SEVEN
Truth: The Third Component of a Teachable Moment 129

CHAPTER EIGHT
The Challenge and Privilege of Being Vulnerable 155

CHAPTER NINE
Milestone Moments 179

CHAPTER TEN
Parents' Questions Answered 203

CHAPTER ELEVEN
101 Common Opportunities for Uncommon Teaching 211

Resource List 245

Acknowledgments

I would like to thank the wise and wonderful people who offered me a slice of their life. I especially thank those professional writers who gave me their "gems," their livelihood, free of charge. I thank Larry Weeden for the opportunity to learn about the art of crafting a nonfiction book; I thank Jim Weidmann for being an example of a loving, caring, and godly parent. I thank Peggy Wilber for her passion, friendship, and humility, and for teaching me just how valuable good relationships are.

Without the support of my family, I would not have had the opportunity to write this book, and I thank them for their sacrifices. I thank Danielle for making her own lunch and doing her homework without being asked; I thank Doug for the many nights he put Justin and Kendrick to bed so that I could keep working, and for his valuable criticisms of the first drafts. I thank wonder-teen Nicole Shughart and grandparents Lottie and Karl Hering for the dozens of hours they spent baby-sitting so that the twins would be in a loving, safe environment. And I thank Justin and Kendrick for not burning down the house while I was taping those unscheduled phone interviews.

I want to acknowledge that anything of truth or value in this book is the work of the Holy Spirit. Anything in this book that is not of virtue is a result of my failure to listen and respond to His prompting. For those errors, I apologize.

—mkh

Introduction

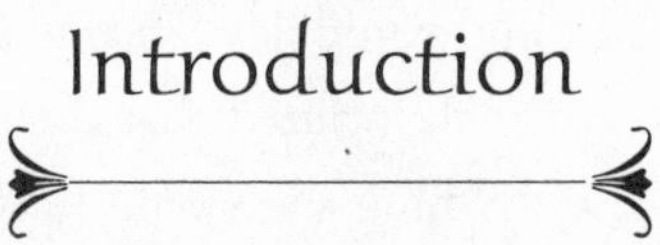

Stephen King couldn't come up with a worse nightmare: On August 20, 2002, my daughter started middle school. *Public* middle school.

I never thought it would happen to me. You see, I quit my job as editor of Focus on the Family's *Clubhouse* magazine in 1996 to be with Danielle, then age five. I wanted to be a full-time, home-schooling, bread-baking, stay-at-home mother, AKA "Super Christian Mom." Well, the bread baking lasted only one day, but I really thought I was going to home school for the long haul, all the way through medical school if need be.

For three years I was on a home-school honeymoon. I loved every day with Danielle. I read the books she read. I chose the friends she had and how much time she spent with each one. I determined which Bible verses she knew and which she didn't (like those about Lot's daughters). We memorized the books of the Bible, did Abeka curriculum, and prayed together every day.

Home school equaled parental control. Home school meant heavy exposure to biblical principles. Home school was my version of heaven on earth.

Then on July 10, 1998, the word *uh-oh* began to define the next phase of my life. That was the kind, sensitive phrase the nurse in the ob-gyn's office used when she saw the ultrasound image of my womb. Uh-oh—two syllables, two tiny babies.

Those babies grew, and grew, and grew, and finally were delivered on February 26, 1999, and though I'm thankful to have two healthy sons, I haven't stopped saying uh-oh since.

Danielle was smack in the middle of second grade when her twin brothers were born. I quickly realized that if she continued to stay home for school, the only thing she would learn is that baby poop comes in Technicolor. The next fall she entered third grade at the public elementary school around the corner from our house.

Fast forward three years and some 11,000 diapers. Danielle leaves for middle school around 8:15 A.M. After all her extracurricular activities are over, she's home at six o'clock, or, if it's a soccer practice night, at seven. Then comes homework while I pour the bowl of Cheerios (ahem, I mean provide a healthy and nutritious, vitamin-rich supper). Next the trumpet sounds, literally, as she practices for band. Soon it's time to put the twins to bed. After I have given them baths, read the entire series of Curious George stories, had a pillow fight, sung several choruses of "I Know an Old Lady Who Swallowed a Fly," prayed with them, and kissed them goodnight, Danielle has been asleep for at least an hour.

My husband, Doug, manages to lead the family through a study on Psalms, though not as routinely as we'd like. He also helps Danielle with her homework when he's not teaching night classes at a local university. We do pull into church nearly every week, 15 minutes late, and send Danielle to Sunday school, but it's still not enough. What exactly is she learning in there while we're singing praise choruses at the opposite end of the building?

That's when I think, I couldn't pick her locker partner out of a lineup. I can't talk to her in the car because we're in a carpool. I can't talk to her in the morning because the twins are awake and screaming for their frozen French toast sticks. I have no idea what she's learning in school. I have no idea who her new friends are. I haven't seen the textbooks because they're not allowed to come home. I can't remember the last time we've studied the Bible together. I can't remember being so out of touch.

Good-bye, Super Christian Mom. Hello, uh-oh.

About the time Danielle entered middle school, I received a call from my friend and former coworker Larry Weeden: Would I be interested in co-authoring a book with Jim Weidmann, the guru of family nights, on a surefire method of training godly kids?

I almost said no because I write primarily "short stuff"—works for short people (kids) or short magazine articles that take short periods of time to write. The last book I actually managed to finish since the twins were born is a phonic reader with only 100 words. I also create a lot of fiction, and the proposed book had to be true.

But I was captivated by the teachable-moments concept. I thought the method could be my answer to the uh-oh situation I'm in—the same situation many parents are in. While I had used teachable moments off and on over the years, I had by no means used them as a methodical, reliable method of spiritual training.

But after catching Jim Weidmann's vision, I realized that teachable moments could be orchestrated to foster Danielle's spiritual growth and that I needed them to happen more often. I also found that even though I couldn't spend the hours with her that I wanted to, I could still take hold of those blocks of time I had with Danielle and impart a meaningful spiritual heritage. I could learn how to build a better relationship that would help us discuss those deeper issues; I could make sure she understood the core values of the Christian life. The ideas also got me thinking about how to be more intentional about teaching the twins, who aren't quite ready for formal Bible training.

So I began to research and write this book, gleaning insights from Heritage Builders Jim Weidmann and Kurt Bruner, as well as from old friends and new. And lo and behold, I found myself thinking, Good-bye, uh-oh. Hello, hope.

—Marianne K. Hering, September 28, 2002

Warning

The families and their stories in this book are true. They do not, however, represent the whole truth. The examples presented here are, for the most part, victory stories of parents whom the Lord has blessed with something likened to success in raising their children. The parents quoted in this book have made many mistakes along the way, but those failures are not noteworthy—nor do we have enough volumes to print them all!

The parents here would like to be remembered for their positive examples in the same way sports figures are remembered for their successes. In 1927 Babe Ruth led the league with 60 home runs, and he also led the league with a total of 89 strikeouts. People didn't flock to Yankee stadium to watch Babe Ruth strike out. They paid money to see him hit home runs.

CHAPTER ONE

What Is a Teachable Moment?

John Benge knew the site would look desolate. The firefighters had told him the house was gone. But he wasn't prepared for the physical shock of seeing his home of 22 years in a heap of charred rubble. His breath grew short; his throat tightened; the tears flowed. The only things left intact were five plastic lawn chairs and the garden hose, which dangled ghostlike from the spigot.

As John inspected the grounds with his 17-year-old son, Austin, he could no longer deny the truth: His family had not a single earthly treasure left—no restored antique cars, no oil painting of the English family home, not one of his daughter's kindergarten drawings. Everything of sentimental and monetary value had been destroyed by a capricious inferno named the Hayman fire, which in 2002 consumed 137,000 acres of Colorado forest, including John's acre lot and his log cabin home.

Father and son sat on the stone steps that used to lead to the log house, steps where the pair had often gazed at the stars and talked. They'd discussed teachers, girls, cars, the future, and God; they pondered the mysteries of the universe on those steps and together had found peace.

This day the mystery they pondered was why God had allowed their home to be consumed while neighboring cabins hadn't even been singed. What was the purpose of their loss?

Austin sat on the familiar steps and absentmindedly played with a loose rock tucked into one of the corners of a step. Underneath it lay a note:

> I just wanted you to know that you are in our thoughts and prayers. Our hearts go out to you and we feel your loss with you. Philippians 4:13—"I can do all things through Christ, which strengthens me." Love in Christ, Doug, an Alaskan firefighter.

The short letter was what they needed to confirm that God's hand was on the whole situation. "I guess we still have everything that's important: family, friends, and God," John said.

"We'll have Christ forever," Austin said. "Nothing else lasts." In that moment, John knew Austin's faith had been tried by fire and had withstood the test.

Christian parents across North America want to know what it takes to build a lasting faith in their children, a faith that can withstand the trials and temptations of this world. They ask, "What can I do to make sure my kids stay strong in the faith—that they pass the test?"

Of course, there is no magic formula, but there are some things parents can do to help develop strong children. Many parents know that the best faith-learning takes place in the context of real life, because it is real life that tests faith. John and Austin will remember the events following the fire and the lessons they learned far longer than they will remember any three-point Sunday sermon. Those precious minutes on the steps of their burned-down cabin represent a faith-learning principle called a "teachable moment."

Capturing a teachable moment is one of the easiest methods to train your child in spiritual matters. These are moments when you are with your child and something occurs that offers an opportunity to teach something about God. It's as simple as paying attention to the world around you and presenting it from a godly viewpoint.

For example, if you see a beautiful tree growing near a lake or river, you can point it out and say to your child, "Isn't that tree magnificent? God says that people of faith are like that tree. Trees stay strong because they grow near the water. People stay strong when they grow closer to God. What other good things happen if you grow near God?"

Or if you are at the grocery store and you receive extra change back from the cashier, you point out the mistake to your child, saying, "God wants us to be people of integrity. Should I give this extra money back or should I keep it?"

If you're like most parents, you want your children to learn biblical principles and become spiritually aware of what God is doing in their lives. And you probably already know that lectures don't work, Sunday school lays a good foundation but isn't always memorable or life-changing, and family devotion time turns into family demoralization time if the material isn't fun and relevant.

Once you discover the power of the teachable moment, however, you will have a method to make a life-changing spiritual impact through everyday events. A teachable moment gives you the resource to make the Bible relevant to your children today, right now, this very moment.

A teachable moment requires three simple ingredients. The first is a good relationship between the parent and child. Most positive learning occurs best inside a loving bond. Second, a teachable moment requires a catalyst such as the fire, the beautiful tree, or the extra change in the examples above. A catalyst is the conversation starter, the reason the teachable moment is occurring at that specific time and place. You can even design your own catalyst to teach your child a specific truth. Third, a teachable moment requires a biblical truth. The truth can be a Bible fact, a truth about God's character, or insights into living a life of faith.

Teachable moments can be used to affirm, encourage, correct, or equip your child in spiritual matters. They are the perfect way to catch your child doing something good. For example, if your child's teacher comments that he gets along well with other people, you can tell him later, "I'm proud of you for being a cooperative person at school. The Bible says that Jesus got along well with other people when he was young. You are following in His footsteps when you treat others with respect and kindness."

Teachable moments are perfect for the single parent who doesn't have a partner to help pass on a spiritual legacy. They can be incorporated into any family routine, no matter how busy. Teachable moments

A Hot Topic

During the summer of 2002, forest fires devastated the western United States. The Hayman fire had counterparts all over Colorado, Arizona, California, and several other states as well. I thought our house in the suburbs, with its green lawn, was safe—that is until one Friday night in July when our next-door neighbor's juniper caught fire. In a matter of seconds, the 20-foot tree blazed like the Olympic torch and quickly caught the garage and nearby bushes on fire. Only the rapid response by neighbors kept the house from burning to the ground and the fire spreading to our home. My daughter, Danielle, witnessed the blaze, and the sight and smell of the small inferno is seared into her memory.

The forest fires had been burning for months. On windy days ash filled the air, and the sunsets glowed deep orange because of the smoky air. But I never thought to use the fires as a teaching tool until a small one struck require no manuals, discussion guides, or preparation. In fact, they work best when you're just having plain old fun with your kids.

Take Just a Moment

Austin Benge didn't suddenly become the kind of person who could trust God in the face of a disaster. His father had carefully nurtured his son's spiritual life to the point where Austin was ready to respond to the loss of his possessions with peace instead of bitterness. John had built a relationship with Austin and throughout his son's life had taught him about the loving nature of God. They'd shared hobbies, including the restoration of antique British cars, and spent many hours together working, playing, and talking. The fire took the cars, but it couldn't touch the special relationship that had been built between father and son; neither could it hurt the relationship between Austin

close to home. After inspecting the destruction of the fire, I read Danielle these verses from James 3:5-6: "Consider what a great forest is set on fire by a small spark. The tongue also is a fire, a world of evil among the parts of the body. It corrupts the whole person, sets the whole course of his life on fire, and is itself set on fire by hell."

As Danielle enters middle school, I know she will see many a social forest fire kindled by the words of friends and classmates. I used this nearby fire as an example of what cruel words can do and how sin, once burning, is difficult to control. Now we have a life event and biblical base to discuss and deal with the inevitable gossip she will encounter. Because of that discussion, she has the Bible as a base for her personal standards of conduct. We never would have had that conversation if the fire hadn't sparked our interest in the Scriptures.

—mkh

and his heavenly Father. Austin's faith had been built up moment by moment with his father, and those faith-learning moments, when added together, will yield him an eternity in heaven with Christ.

You can have the same type of spiritual influence on your children. The chapters of this book will allow you to discover the impact of teachable moments and how to shape them. You'll be able to understand the dynamics of teachable moments and to recognize those golden opportunities when they arise. Finally, this book will give you tools and ideas on how to create your own teachable moments. You'll know *what* to teach your children, *when* to do it, and *how* to make those moments spiritually meaningful.

We hope these pages will inspire you to keep your children's spiritual development a top priority. As a result of using the teachable moments God provides each day, your relationship with your children will be strong and spiritually rich. We want you to grasp and share the joy that God has for your family every waking moment.

Jim Weidmann
Marianne K. Hering

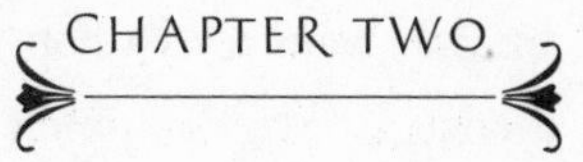

Being Available—A Matter of Priorities

Children grow up at warp speed. One second you're dreading that midnight feeding and fretting about the cost of diapers and then *swoosh*—you're in a different galaxy. The kids are gone, and you're having a garage sale, selling the roller hockey goals, the bunk beds, and six boxes of Beanie Babies.

Where did the time go? Wasn't it just yesterday you were fiddling with the car seat and helping tie their shoes?

Consider this opening soliloquy taken from *Father of the Bride* (1991). Character George Banks expresses his loss only hours after his daughter's wedding: "I remember how her little hand used to fit inside mine. How she used to love to sit on my lap and lean her head against my chest.... I was her hero.... Before you know it, you're sitting in a big empty house wearing rice on your tux, wondering what happened to your life."

We can learn the value of spending time with children from grandparents, who have the perspective gained from experience. They know just how precious each moment with a child is and have a knack for finding ways to develop close relationships with their grandchildren. Nancy Parker Brummett, known as "Grancy" to her grandchildren, tells about her close relationship with her granddaughter Francesca:

> When my first granddaughter was born, I had a very special necklace made to commemorate the event. It was a gold cross with a small diamond chip in the center. My plan was to wear it until she turned 21, then give it to her as an heirloom.
>
> When Francesca was just a baby, she'd reach for the cross around my neck, pull it to her mouth, and slobber all over it. As she got older, she'd sit on my lap and look for the chain so she could pull the cross out of my blouse and look at it. "This is going to be my cross someday, isn't it, Grancy?" she would say. My heirloom-building plan was working beautifully! That is, until the summer before Francesca turned six. I had gone to visit her and her family. We were sightseeing in Creede, Colorado, when I realized my necklace was no longer around my neck. The safety clasp must have come undone. I was devastated. "But that was supposed to be my cross, Grancy," Francesca said as we searched the sidewalks leading back to where we had parked the car, and I thought my heart would break. When I saw that she was getting more upset each time she looked at my face, however, I realized I was sending her the wrong message. After all, the cross was special, but it was still just an object. Finally, she and I sat down on a bench in front of a rustic general store in Creede. "I'll get another cross to give you, honey," I said. "Will it have a diamond, Grancy?" she asked with excitement. "No, I don't think so," I answered after some prompting from the Holy Spirit. "Now I know that you're my precious jewel, so I don't need one with a diamond. And you know what else? As long as we have each other, we shouldn't be so sad about losing the cross. The Bible tells us people are more important than things." That

talk and a couple of ice cream cones made us both feel much better. Driving home, I realized that my initial grief at losing the cross—and it did feel like grief—was not because of the value I placed in it, but because of how much I was looking forward to giving it to Francesca. In Acts 20:35, Paul quotes Jesus as having said, "It is more blessed to give than to receive." We know that's true from the joy we experience by giving. I look forward to giving Francesca more than just a necklace that will one day be lost or destroyed; I hope to help pass on a spiritual heritage she will keep throughout eternity.

It's About Time ...

Several years ago, *Clubhouse* magazine asked kids to send in ideas for helpful inventions to give their dads. The editors expected to receive some wacky suggestions for golf gizmos or automatic nose hair pluckers, but what poured in were ideas for machines that would do Dad's work so he could be at home more often. What was intended as a lighthearted question revealed that the readers had heavy hearts: The children longed to spend more time with their fathers.

Britney, age eight, from Bumpass, Virginia, wrote: "With this carpenter machine, my dad can take a day off and send this robot to work." An 11-year-old physician's son said, "I would invent a robot surgeon to help my dad get his work done more quickly so he can come home earlier." And the most poignant of the lot: "Since I am not around to give my dad hugs, I would create a gizmo that would give him hugs and make him feel good."

The letters were from kids probably a lot like yours, Christian kids who just want more attention. Eleven-year-old Paige of Cranston, Rhode Island, wrote: "My dad is a pastor, so he is very busy on Saturdays making his sermon. I would make him an invention that writes his sermons for him." The responses *Clubhouse* received were aimed at dads because it was a Father's Day issue, but kids need their moms, too. Because an estimated 72 percent of mothers with children under age 18 work outside the home, we can assume that children would create similar work-reducing inventions so that Mom can also have more time at home.

Our children need and want time with both their parents. Are you there for yours? To assess your baseline Availability Score, take this short quiz about the last seven days' family activities. If you're a parent with a job that requires travel, or a divorced parent with only partial custody, modify the time span to reflect the last week you lived with your child or, if you see him or her only on weekends, the last month.

1. I ate at least three meals with my children last week.

   ___Yes ___No

2. During the last seven days, I made sure that I spent at least one hour alone with each of my children.

   ___Yes ___No

3. I can tell you what clothes my children wore yesterday (without searching the laundry basket or looking under their beds for clues).

   ___Yes ___No

4. If I asked my children right now, they would say that last week we had at least one fun family time together.

   ___Yes ___No

5. The last time I ran errands, I took a child with me.

   ___Yes ___No

6. In the last seven days I helped my oldest child with a hobby, homework, or sports activity.

   ___Yes ___No

7. I tucked my youngest child into bed at least twice this week.

   ___Yes ___No

8. I went on a "date" with one of my children last week.

   ___Yes ___No

9. I have given each of my children at least three compliments over the last seven days.

 ___Yes ___No

10. My children know about and are looking forward to our next scheduled family activity.

 ___Yes ___No

11. I know the names of each of my children's "best" friends this week, and I know the names of the people they ate lunch with.

 ___Yes ___No

12. I know the names of my children's Sunday school teachers as well as their academic teachers.

 ___Yes ___No

13. I hugged each of my children every day last week.

 ___Yes ___No

Tally the number of "yes" answers and check out your score:
0 to 4: Is this a hint that you may not be spending enough time with your children?
5 to 9: You probably clock in enough hours at home, but you may need to intentionally develop your parent-child relationships. Pay special attention to the section titled "Questions Are Better Than Answers" in chapter 4.
10 to 13: You're there; you're doing the right things. Good job.

Mind Your P's and Q's

If you want to make a spiritual impact on your child, you need to know the answer to the old riddle—**Q:** How do you spell love? **A:** T-I-M-E.

As we saw from the *Clubhouse* letters, all kids need a certain quantity of time to feel connected to their parents. But there's another "Q" word to consider: quality. This parenting buzzword has been flying around for several years, stinging parents who are home but don't interact with their children. The gist of the concept is that it doesn't really matter how much parents are home as long as the time spent with their children is "quality" time—meaning that parents and children are engaged in some relationship-building activity. Conscientious parents can plan that spectacular, special quality time with their children and then not worry about whether they are able to help with homework.

But at some point common sense must tell you that the "quality" concept breaks down if there isn't enough time and effort put into a relationship with your child. Sure, you can plan and take a wonderful two-week vacation to Orlando, Florida, but that doesn't mean you can blow off the wind ensemble concert or skate clear of hockey commitments.

On the other side of the "Q" question is whether quantity can replace quality. The answer is no. Letting your children watch TV for

Laser Lesson

I had a rare free Saturday afternoon. My daughter had a rare free coupon for the nearby laser tag arena.

"Sure, I'd love to play laser tag with you," I told Danielle. As I said the words, I found I actually meant them, even though I had also wanted to get some work done or take a bike ride.

After the laser tag game and reviewing my score card, she said, "Look, Mom, you're only 160 points behind the guy in first place. Next time maybe you'll move up to the top ten."

Danielle had placed third out of 28 players.

"Do you think I'll ever win?" I asked.

"Mom, be serious. You'll never be first if I'm playing against you."

No, I thought, *I'm already in first place. As long as you want to spend time with me, I've won the game.*

—mkh

hours while you're surfing the Net is not the right approach either. Raising kids is a daily performance, and you have top billing on the marquee. To build a healthy relationship with your child, especially a healthy spiritual relationship, you need to supply quality time in a healthy quantity.

In his book *Home with a Heart*, Dr. James Dobson, founder of Focus on the Family, gives this illustration:

> Let's suppose you've looked forward all day to eating at one of the finest restaurants in town. The waiter brings you a menu, and you order the most expensive steak in the house. But when the meal arrives, you see a tiny piece of meat about one inch square in the middle of the plate. When you complain about the size of the steak, the waiter says, "Sir, I recognize that the portion is small, but that's the finest corn-fed beef money can buy. You'll never find a better bite of meat than we've served you tonight. As to the portion, I hope you understand that it's not the quantity that matters, it's the quality that counts."
>
> You would object, and for good reason. Why? Because both quality and quantity are important in many areas of our lives, including how we relate to children. They need our time and the best we have to give them.
>
> My concern is that the quantity versus quality argument might be a poorly disguised rationalization for giving our children—neither.

The key to balancing the "Q" words is "P" for priority. If parents don't make their children a top priority in time or effort, eventually it will show. Usually, the first ones to realize something is wrong are the kids themselves. Children can see through a father who offers a token afternoon at the miniature golf course but doesn't take the time to show up at baseball games or help with spelling homework. Even if a mother buys expensive clothes and toys for them, her children feel that she really doesn't care if she's not around when they're sad or need someone to talk to. The mother or father who is home but engaged in their own pursuits instead of the pursuits of their children will be exposed when their children grow resentful and emotionally distant.

How much time is enough? Just how much interaction do kids really need? Why not ask your children? Like the *Clubhouse* readers, they'll tell you if they need more time or attention.

Hmmm. You don't have that kind of rapport with your children? They wouldn't talk to you about that? Maybe you need to consider entering their world and seeing things from their perspective. Spend time with your children to find out what's important to them. You may find out you have more in common than you thought.

Family Style

My (Marianne's) husband, Doug, was laid off from his finance job with a software developer just 32 days before September 11, 2001, when the heart and economy of our country took a hit. I had to scramble and get back to work to help pay the bills. It was an adjustment for me because, before then, my children and husband had consumed most of my emotional resources. I didn't know how much work I could squeeze in without squeezing them out.

Because I'm a writer, I must juggle my time between deadlines and family demands. If I make enough money on a project, I "buy" family time by eating out more often and hiring a housecleaner. Most days I limit the number of hours my preschool twins spend in daycare to three. But no matter how early I get up or how late I burn the midnight oil working, every once in a while I must work more daytime hours than I'd like.

I have a gauge that tells me if I've been too wrapped up in work: the bed. The latest my children are allowed to stay up is 9 P.M. If at

9:30 my bed has only pillows and sheets on it, then I know my husband has succeeded in getting them off to dreamland. Many times, however, I come upstairs to find my bed occupied by small visitors. Either my daughter is wrapped up in the sheets or the twins are having a pillow fight.

For one reason or another, Dad just can't get them to settle down and go to sleep. They need more Mom and can't relax without their "fix." So they go to the place where they're most likely to find me at night. My daughter usually wants to talk about the day or her friends. For the most part, she just needs to know that I want to listen. One son always needs Mommy's cuddles and kisses. The other has some burning question that only I can answer, such as "Do kitties like asparagus?"

On those nights, I stay with them until they fall asleep and then move them to their own beds. Next day, I may spend extra time with the twins doing crafts or making sure I'm the one to help Danielle with her math homework. I make adjustments.

Another change I had to make was to schedule dates with Danielle. Because her brothers are seven years younger, our family activities are geared toward the preschool set. The most sophisticated movies we rent for the family are those old-fashioned Disney greats like *The Love Bug.* Danielle enjoys those times, but she would rather be doing things that are more age-appropriate. Actually, we all need a little time away from the three-year-olds. Their high energy makes everyone a little nutty, not to mention that their constant chatter makes having a deep conversation difficult.

Enter the schedule: Once a week, either Doug or I commit to taking Danielle out for some sort of food treat and an activity. It can be anything from a bike ride to a Christian concert. Now, Danielle even plans and schedules the events for us. She knows when and where we are going and reminds us so we don't forget. What started as our priority is now hers as well.

Make No Excuses

Meaningful family time is a priority with most kids, even teens, though some don't show it. Helping teens figure out their family dynamics is a standard topic addressed by magazines aimed at adolescents. Let's take a moment to enter that world and view family life from their perspective. In a recent issue of a secular teen magazine, the editors categorized different types of parents and asked their readers to find the ones that fit their families. The list of parenting styles that follows is based on and adapted from that article.

Teachable Moments Remembered #1

- "My mom and I had many late-into-the-night discussions while sitting on my bed. She was not afraid to answer any of my questions, and no concern or frustration was too silly for her. She laughed with me, cried with me—she made me feel valuable by just wanting to be with me. These times laid a foundation of trust that made me want to ask about more spiritual matters."
- "My dad, brother, and I went to breakfast together at least once a week throughout high school. We didn't always have a serious discussion, but it was nice to know we would have that time together to talk or even just to laugh."
- "Even though my dad was not always a huge spiritual influence when I was growing up, I remember the few times that were instrumental. When I was in about second grade, we owned a country store out in the middle of nowhere. In order to have Sunday morning papers on hand for customers, my dad had to leave about half past four in the morning to pick them up. He asked each of us children at different times to go along with him, and then he would take us out to breakfast."
- "My dad would always talk to me man-to-man anytime we rode together, even when it was only six minutes to get home."

- **The Wallet**—the parent who is never there but always has a lot of money because of all the overtime he or she puts in.
- **The Ghost**—you never know when or where this parent is going to show up.
- **The Tennis Racket**—this parent makes sure his or her personal needs are being met. As a result, he or she pursues personal enrichment and leaves the kids emotionally poor.
- **The Pew**—the parent who has time to help at or attend every church function but never the time to help at home.
- **The Party**—this parent has so many friends, committee meetings, and social functions that he or she doesn't have time to be friends with his or her own children.

This list represented the parents who needed to do some work on their time-management skills. (There were some healthier choices included in the list, and we'll meet those parents in chapter 5.) It's sad to realize that teens can skim this list and without even hesitating declare, "That's my dad" or "My mom's just like The Tennis Racket."

Yes, this list is cynical and a little shallow. Children can't really explain life from a mature perspective, which is exactly why they need your time and guidance. Children can do little but become cynical if their parents don't want to put effort into the relationship, but there is something you can do if you recognize your mode of operation in the list above and want to have a better parent-child bond.

You can change your priorities.

Single parent and radio host Bobbie Lemieux tells about her recent change of "station":

> I love my chosen profession—broadcasting—but I love my daughter more. After being a traffic reporter for 12 months, I landed a job as a morning host for the local Christian radio station. In broadcasting, I was meeting my professional goals as well as exciting and influential people. I became a local

celebrity of sorts, and I seemed to have a dream job. So why wasn't I walking "on air"?

After a year or so, bringing home a paycheck as a radio announcer was costing too much. The hours were lousy; I had to leave the house at 4:30 A.M. and oftentimes had to work full weekends. As a single mother, I felt I was spending too much time away from my daughter, Martha. Additionally, the stress of such a demanding work environment left me with little energy. Being on the air drained away what little emotional resources I had. The turning point came when Martha's first-grade teacher sent back homework that wasn't done correctly, homework that I had supervised. Hey, I'm definitely not functioning at full capacity! I have a college degree in journalism, and I can't even figure out a first-grade language arts worksheet?! I needed a new job.

After praying and looking around a bit, I was offered a position as a mortgage broker by one of the radio station's advertisers. Becoming a financial "expert" was totally out of my area of experience. Besides buying my own house, I had never contemplated selling home loans; it seemed as far out of my sphere as being a brain surgeon. Plus, the job was paid on commission; what if I didn't sell any loans? But the Lord let me know it was the right career path at the moment. The training was short; the hours were flexible. I could sleep in on Saturdays and spend the day with Martha.

Soon I was selling enough loans to stay financially afloat without sinking emotionally. Less than a year after taking this step of faith to be home more with Martha, God brought me back to broadcasting as a morning host with a different station. This time, however, the hours are shorter and the work is less demanding. I come home energized instead of drained. I have stripped my life to the bare essentials—work and Martha. God has been wonderful. He has taken care of the details. Martha even passed first grade!

The 24-Hour Puzzle

God created all parents equal. They are each given 24 hours every day. The parents of every famous godly person you can think of from Timothy to Mother Teresa—all of those parents had the same amount of time to raise their children. God knows what you need to equip your children, and He will faithfully provide it. Scripture says, "God will meet all your needs according to his glorious riches in Christ Jesus" (Philippians 4:19). That includes the necessary time.

One mantra of the twentieth century was "I need to find time to...." Everyone wanted to "find" time to be home with the kids, exercise, read more, learn to cook Chinese food, research better stock investments, play golf, or build a dream house in the mountains. On occasion a parent can buy time, but no one ever finds it—you have to make it. Time is a lot like money: Once you spend it, it's gone, but if you invest time wisely, it'll pay dividends in the future.

Here are some common time-snatchers that steal away the resources that could belong to your children.

• **House Beautiful:** Yes, you need to keep your home orderly to create a positive atmosphere. No, you don't have to compete with Martha Stewart when your children live at home. Some people, especially women, feel that their house is a reflection of who they are, and if the house isn't "perfect," they keep trying to make it so. Let the house go and make it a home! Work on encouraging your children to reflect Christ and seek perfectionism in spiritual things. In the long term, that will bring your home more honor than creating a house suited for the cover of *Better Homes & Gardens*.

• **Sports:** "Physical training is of some value," according to 1 Timothy 4:8, "but godliness has value for all things, holding promise for both the present life and the life to come." Get up early to do your workouts, before the kids are awake. Or run away from your physical addictions—they won't pay off at the end of life's marathon, but raising your children will. If you're not under doctor's orders, cut back your sports training time to a health-maintenance level. To avoid being known as The Tennis Racket, you can pick up sports again when your children are old enough to enjoy it with you or when they are gone; the masters divisions and senior leagues will be there waiting for you.

• **Hobbies:** Right now, the best hobbyhorse to ride is the one your kids can ride with you. Unless your child can participate, cut back on time spent with the model trains, turn off the Internet, put away the paintbrushes—for now. You can dabble in those pursuits later, when your kids are in school or college. Teen expert and camp director Joe

Always Take a Kid Along

"Hey, Jake. Put your shoes on. Let's get going."

"Okay, Dad."

It's Saturday, errand day for Dad. The van needs an oil change. Then there's a trip to the hardware store for screws and pipes and gadgets for the latest home improvement project: the perfect time for a one-on-one with one of the kids.

My dad taught me that. "Never go anywhere without a child," he told me. And he's right. By taking a kid away from the siblings, I get his or her full attention, and the child gets mine. I'm building the relationship while setting up the impromptu times. These are the moments when life presents questions either from me or from my child, and the answers come from our faith view. The principle is that I must develop the relationship, for the relationship gives me the ability to share spiritual truth.

—J.W.

White recommends that hobby enthusiasts "make your children your hobby."

• **Work:** Are you The Wallet? If you can't keep your hours down at your current job, call a headhunter and seek a new career path. Some breadwinners, especially single parents without child support, feel tied to their employment since that job represents their only means of financial sustenance. Those parents need to pray that God will intervene and provide a way for them to earn enough money and be at home when needed. For others, the issue isn't money. It's a noble goal to house, feed, and clothe your children, but let's face it: Some of you go way beyond the call of duty. Can you cut back on your work without jeopardizing your livelihood? Take the matter to the Lord in prayer. Seek His guidance in this all-important decision, and listen and obey if He directs a change.

• **Ministry:** "[The overseer] must manage his own family well and see that his children obey him with proper respect. (If anyone does not know how to manage his own family well, how can he take care of God's church?) A deacon...must manage his children and his household well" (1 Timothy 3:4-5, 12). This passage explains that believers who want to be in charge or have ministry responsibilities must be good family people. The things you learn by being a good parent, for example, building relationships and managing priorities, transfer to ministry. If you want to serve God well, start by serving your family well. In time, God will show you when and where you are to minister to others. Several ministry possibilities exist that can include your whole family. During this phase of your life, why not pursue those? Otherwise, the moniker The Pew may stick to you.

• **Stuff and More Stuff:** Lower your standard of living to raise your child-rearing standard. Simplify. Simplify. Simplify. If you can do with fewer things, you'll have more for your children in the way of relationship time. A large house requires large amounts of energy in terms of repairs, yard work, headaches, and emotional strain. Or do you spend a lot of time and emotional energy watching the stock market? Consolidate investments and let your money take care of you, not the other way around. Get rid of those material possessions that drain your relationship resources. Be careful that what you purchase for your children doesn't consume them. Luke 12:15 says, "A man's life does not consist in the abundance of his possessions." What do you want your child's life to consist of?

• **Social Events:** Are you a social butterfly who needs to crawl back into the cocoon? It's fine and healthy to have adult relationships, but consider meeting your friends for lunch instead of an entire evening. Or go on family outings with other families; that way everyone can socialize together. Want to join a professional organization? Perhaps you can find one with monthly meetings instead of weekly commitments. That way you won't be known as The Party. If you're an extrovert, spend time with your children and their friends. Welcome

Rest in Peace

When Alfred Nobel was 55 years old, he awoke one morning to read his obituary in the newspaper. (His brother Ludwig had died, and the newspaper ran the obituary for the wrong Nobel.) This brilliant scientist, who had invented practical uses for dynamite and nitroglycerin, read that he was a "merchant of death," a man who had made an immense fortune from the development and sales of "weapons for destruction." He was horrified this was the way the world saw him, that his life could be summed up in one derogatory sentence.

Nobel had erroneously believed that if weapons of mass destruction were created, war would cease. He speculated that if world leaders could produce the verifiable threat of annihilation, they would frighten each other into peaceful negotiation. Unfortunately for Mr. Nobel, his efforts literally and figuratively blew up in his face, and his inventions produced far more deaths than his conscience was comfortable with.

everyone to your home. Finding ways to be around and know your children's friends gives you a special insight into their world.

The sacrifice isn't always easy. When my (Jim's) children were under the age of five, I was heavily involved in church events. My schedule took precedent over my family's activities. I ran the men's breakfast, helped usher, participated in men's Bible studies—and I was on the church baseball team.

But when my oldest son, Joshua, turned five, his outside-the-home life began to blossom. He had Cub Scouts and baseball practice. As his social life grew, mine shrank. The most painful loss was quitting the baseball team; I was the star pitcher, and we had just won the league championship. It was hard to accept that I had to make my "out."

The kids' activities also bit into my wife's sanity time. She was home all day with them, and having to run errands in the evenings too

After reading the untimely obituary, Nobel decided to do something to change his reputation and shape the world for the peace he so desired—a true priority in his life. After his real death some eight years later, his will birthed the concept and funds for the Nobel prizes for peace. Mr. Nobel stopped merely longing for peace; he did something about it.

Like Alfred Nobel, every person alive has time to change his or her obituary. If the man who held the patent for the explosive nitrocellulose can become known as a peacemaker, then parents can also change their priorities to reflect their true heartfelt passion—their children. You can change the way your children see you by changing your actions. Even if your previous good intentions and efforts have "blown up" in your face, with God's help, you can turn your passion for your children into a practical priority. It's not too late.

—mkh

got to be draining. As I was coming in the front door to watch the kids, she was going out.

"Where you going?" I'd ask.

"Anywhere," she'd say.

"When you coming home?"

"I don't know...."

I oftentimes failed miserably as my own agenda would keep my resources tied up, and I know my wife missed out on a lot of the activities she enjoyed. After setting aside time for God and our marriage, however, we teamed up to make sure that the children came first for this season in our lives. Everything else could wait.

Good Conversation

Okay, so now you've made some time to spend with your children; many of you, in fact, have managed to gather quite a bit of time. The average American child between the ages of three and 12 spends about 31 hours a week with their mother and 23 hours with their father, according to researchers at the University of Michigan. That's about four and a half hours per day with Mom, and about three with Dad. What are you going to do with all that time you've made? What will you talk about? What do your children want to talk about? What meaningful conversations does God want you to have with your children?

In a 2001 study titled "Grading Grown-Ups," the Lutheran Brotherhood, along with the Search Institute, determined that "though 75 percent of adults say it is important to have meaningful conversations with children and youth, just 34 percent of adults actually have such conversations." It's not enough to desire meaningful conversations; parents have to make them happen. But how?

Deuteronomy 6:6-7 says, "These commandments that I give you today are to be upon your hearts. Impress them on your children.

Talk about them when you sit at home and when you walk along the road, when you lie down and when you get up." Basically, all of life is an opportunity to develop your children's spiritual outlook or mindset.

You might say that's not possible, and it may sound burdensome. But with just a little effort, most parents can come a lot closer to the mark than they think. Grasping the power of the teachable moment will allow you naturally to work God into everyday conversations. Teachable moments are fun, simple, and effective ways to impress your children with God's truth. They can be used virtually anywhere—the kitchen, the carpool, on vacation, or at the mall. It's time to take advantage of the spur of the teachable moments that come along.

Sometimes kids experience a spiritual growth spurt at big, monumental events: a Young Life rally, a Billy Graham crusade, a week at church camp, a short-term missions trip with the youth group. Those can, indeed, be powerful times of strengthening commitment to God. But most often, growth occurs in the less significant, more mundane moments of everyday life, when Mom and Dad are there to talk about faith and the nitty-gritty stuff of life as it happens.

If we want to help our children grow consistently, we'll take advantage of all those day-in, day-out opportunities: driving to school and soccer practice, working together around the house, eating pizza at home on Friday night, throwing the Frisbee around at the park, cleaning out an elderly neighbor's rain gutters. In teachable moments like these, we can talk with our children about life and love, faith and the future.

This is precisely what the writer of Deuteronomy was getting at, and this concept is so important that it is repeated almost verbatim just a few chapters later (see 11:19).

Do these unspectacular, seemingly insignificant moments of faith building really make a difference? Listen as three college students talk about what influenced their lives during the teen years:

Bridgette, age 21

"I have always been a daddy's girl, and I was the only one who could wake up Dad for church. When I was little, I would gently shake him and tickle him. When I got older, I would crawl in bed beside him and use that time to share my heart with him. Everyone else would be rushing to get ready, but Dad and I would lie there for a long time, talking, connecting, and sharing our hopes and dreams. Those times helped me understand so many aspects of my heavenly Father—love, acceptance, gentleness, and compassion.

"My mom did not like to cook much, but when she did, I would go in the kitchen with her and talk. We would share so much about our lives, talking very openly and relating as friends. This didn't occur until I was going through adolescence, and I was able to appreciate all she had given to me and to accept her unconditionally."

James, age 20

"Because I didn't have my own car during high school, my parents drove me everywhere—to youth group, baseball practice, friends' houses. I remember that they really tried to use that time, whether it was a five-minute drive or an hour, to talk about things. They could have turned on the news or a game or stayed in their own world like we all do sometimes when driving. But they always made an effort to ask questions and draw me out. If I was coming home from Bible study, Mom would say, 'What did you learn? What do you think about that?' If I was coming home from school, Dad would say, 'Tell me about your friends' or 'What can I be praying about in your life?'

"Recently, I asked my folks about all those drive-time discussions, and they said, 'We decided early on that if we were going to spend hours each week driving you around, it was going to be time well-spent.' And it sure was. I stayed connected to my parents talking during all those hours in the car."

Heidi, age 21

"My dad has always been busy with work—not out of choice, but out of necessity and the nature of his job. But every year for our birthdays, he has always taken each of us four kids out to breakfast. As we've gotten older, my sister and I have initiated 'breakfast with Dad' more than once a year. They are treasured times when we talk about life, God, the future. Memories are made in quiet cafés in early mornings.

"Growing up in northern Minnesota was an adventure. We heated our house with wood, which meant cutting trees and hauling logs every fall. My dad and my three siblings and I worked side by side, and nobody told us it was hard work and shouldn't be fun. We stacked the cart full of logs, rode on top of the pile, and sang praise songs all the way home. We all made memories and learned the value of hard work without even knowing it."

That line of Heidi's—"Memories are made in quiet cafés in early mornings"—is not only poetic; it's also profoundly true. Each day presents opportunities to explore faith issues and build your relationship with your child. Grab hold of every opportunity you can.

Parenting with a Purpose

On October 30, 1920, Dr. Fred Banting *felt* the cure for diabetes before he could put the idea of it into words. His method for research would be to use the pancreases of healthy dogs to keep diabetic dogs alive. All his colleagues thought him crazy for pursuing a cure for the "sugar sickness," which was slowly starving hundreds of thousands of people to death. The most learned scholars and researchers hadn't even come up with an undisputed theory as to what caused the illness. No one thought Banting had any hope of finding an antidote; he was just a surgeon, a country surgeon at that, and not a very successful one. He had no money, no lab animals, not even a test tube. He had never studied the digestive system or biochemistry. He was basically a stubborn man who had some skill with a surgeon's knife and faith in an idea.

When he finally got a grant, it was for 10 dogs, an assistant, and eight weeks in a chemistry lab. With that, and only that, he was attempting to solve one of medicine's most baffling mysteries of the day.

He had to sell his office furniture and medical instruments to survive. He was a self-appointed, untitled, and utterly broke researcher—but he was determined and had a method.

He began with utter failure. His mistakes and miscalculations

Lessons from a Potato

If you're not sure how to formally teach your children about the Bible, take heart. There are many methods available for passing on your faith. *The Parents' Guide to the Spiritual Mentoring of Teens* suggests parents consider the lowly potato. If the only way you served potatoes was boiled or mashed without any salt, pepper, butter, or gravy, your family would quickly tire of eating them. But if you go through your recipe books, chances are you could come up with a different way to serve potatoes every night of the week, probably for several weeks in a row, and your family would never get sick of them. You could make French fries; potato salad; baked potatoes with sour cream, chives, and bacon bits; even potato pancakes. You'd be using the same basic ingredient every night—potatoes—but the different spices you add and the variety of presentations would keep your family's taste buds begging for more.

In a similar way, spiritual training has a number of basic ingredients (Bible reading, teaching, discussion, prayer) and a single purpose (to develop mature Christians). But just as there are countless ways to serve potatoes, so there are countless ways in which the ingredients of faith training can be combined with the other elements and presented in such a way that each session is challenging, exciting, and rewarding for everyone. Perhaps it's time to change your spiritual training "recipe" and look at new, enjoyable, and exciting ways to train your children in their Christian faith.

The problem may in part be your spiritual comfort zone—the feeling that spiritual things should be presented in a serious and solemn manner, much like they were in Sunday school when you grew up. When you get to choosing what methods and models you will use with your family, make sure you

were costly, but slowly his skill improved, his method became more sure. His research inched along as he kept his diabetic dog specimens alive much longer than was thought medically possible. When the medical community slowly nodded their heads in approval and

decide on the basis of what matches and will work for your family, not on what matches what you've done before or what falls within your comfort zone.

Get resources that help you get the job done (see the list provided in the appendix). There are many books that give ideas for teaching your kids. But there are also videos, software, Web sites, and music and audiocassettes of every description. Vary your tools and approach.

Use your kids' creativity. Even after you've decided on a method and a plan, stay open to creative suggestions and alternative ideas. Give them options and ask them how they would like to approach learning a certain topic or doing family-time learning. They may suggest some off-the-wall things like learning about spiritual warfare by playing laser tag; if you go with it, they'll never forget the experience or the lesson. Never forget that God has given us the gifts of humor and laughter. No matter how dry the activity or lesson, slow down and relax enough to let in some joking around, a little wrestling or tickling with your younger kids, and maybe some humorous storytelling with your older ones. Sometimes you may end up on an entirely different topic, but the time together and the wisdom shared won't be forgotten.

If your children have musical gifts, why not let them use music in their spiritual growth? Have them write a song about God's love or about a particular aspect of their relationship with God and perform it on a family night. If they are artistic, why not encourage them to try to give expression to God's forgiveness by drawing on paper or sculpting with clay? This will establish a connection between your kids' talents and the things of the Spirit.

Get together, talk, and share ideas with others who are intentional about spiritual training.

acknowledged results, Dr. Banting injected the first human patient—himself—with life-saving "isletin," now called insulin.

Every parent needs to tackle child rearing like Fred Banting tackled diabetes. The job of raising godly children requires a great idea, passion for the task, and a method. It doesn't matter if you don't have the right qualifications. It doesn't matter if everyone else thinks you will fail. It doesn't matter if you don't have a lot of money or the right equipment. It only matters that you have faith in God, heartfelt commitment, and a way to go about it.

The Great Idea

The idea, or faith principle, behind godly parenting can be found in Scripture. Let's take a second look at Deuteronomy 6:6-7: "These commandments that I give to you today are to be upon your hearts. Impress them on your children. Talk about them when you sit at home and when you walk along the road, when you lie down and when you get up." This call is for parents—not pastors, Sunday school teachers, or youth workers. It's for moms and dads, and it's for every day and every place.

There is an informal and a formal part to this command. The formal teaching aspect in our culture includes family devotions, curriculum, Sunday school, youth meetings or Bible clubs, and Bible verse memorization. The informal has many different looks, and one method for informal training is the main topic of this book—teachable moments. They are fun, spontaneous, simple, and life-shaping.

The power for a teachable moment's life-changing impact is found in Scripture. The Bible is what creates faith learning. Second Timothy 3:16-17 reminds us that "All Scripture is God-breathed and is useful for teaching, rebuking, correcting and training in righteousness, so that the man of God may be thoroughly equipped for every good work." This doesn't mean that you have to know the exact book and verse your teachable moments stem from. It does mean that spiritual truths have a power to affect your children's souls in a way that other teaching doesn't. For example, the truth that Jesus loves your children and was willing to die for them has much more spiritual impact than teaching them the truth that the earth revolves around the sun. When you use teachable moments for the purpose of faith building, God's truths are an unseen partner helping you in your task.

It's your job to present the material in the best method for the moment; it's up to the Holy Spirit to make it take hold. God's truths are alive and fulfill His purposes. Isaiah 55:10-11 declares:

> As the rain and the snow come down from heaven,
> and do not return to it without watering the earth
> and making it bud and flourish…
> so is my word that goes out from my mouth:
> It will not return to me empty,
> but will accomplish what I desire
> and achieve the purpose for which I sent it.

This takes the pressure off you, Mom and Dad. Presenting biblical truths is your job; making them "bud and flourish" is God's. If you make mistakes or don't see results, it doesn't matter as long as you are obedient and stay with it. Dr. Banting's first efforts didn't come close to resulting in a vial of insulin, but those mistakes shaped his thinking and eventually helped him discover the pathway to isolating the cure. In the same way, each teachable moment might not produce life-changing results, but the method as a whole is sound, and with God's blessing, teachable moments will produce results over time.

The worst teachable moment that I (Jim) can remember presenting was a family night session centered on the concept "Is it okay to be angry with God?" That lesson failed. It flopped. While I talked, my children sat there on the couch with eyes as glazed as Krispy Kreme donuts. I tried to put the lesson out of my mind.

A Hard Loss

I often find comparisons between the sports world and the spiritual world. Part of the reason I support athletic activities for my children is that sports help my children identify faith lessons and learn from them.

Last spring is a good example. My 11-year-old son, Doug, made the last out—a strikeout—in a closely contested baseball game, and he took it hard because he felt he had let the team down. Doug is a good athlete, and he usually excels at all the sports he participates in. He felt his strikeout showed that he was a poor baseball player.

I talked to Doug a day after the game (he was more willing to listen then because the crisis had passed) and explained to him that an unexpected failure like this might be pointing out something he needs to work on. It's not a statement that he is a failure.

This is similar to how we often respond to sin in our lives. Sometimes God brings to light a sin that we were previously unaware of. After discovering the harsh reality that we have sinned or failed, we are brought low by the realization. We can then choose to be hard on ourselves about it or deny that it ever happened. Or instead, we can be humble and view it as an opportunity to identify our weakness and dedicate ourselves to improve in that area.

Doug and I spent some time working on his hitting before the next game, and the extra work paid off. Doug said the practices really helped him in the game, and he realizes he has improved himself, as a ball player, by recognizing his weaknesses and working on them.

My prayer is that in the contest of life, Doug will accept each failure as a challenge.

—anonymous

Three years later, on September 12, 2001, Jacob popped this question on me: "Hey, Dad, is it okay to be angry with God?" Now, I have learned that with Jacob, it's best to let him do the explaining first, since he's got such a good grasp on theology. Sometimes these questions are a test, and if I'm afraid I might fail it, I've learned to say, "Well, Jacob, what do you think?" before I jump in.

This time when I asked him what he thought, he came back and told me the three points of the "failed" family night. The lesson I had tried to put out of my mind had been in the back of his, waiting for the day he could apply it.

Passion for the Task

Parents with a passion for the Bible have an easier time training their children because that passion is contagious and helps keep them motivated. Dr. Banting had a passion for his goal, and he relentlessly pursued it, even to his personal financial loss. Fred Banting isn't famous for what he didn't do about diabetes; he's remembered for what he did do.

Any person off the street would agree to the statement "A good Christian should follow the Ten Commandments." It's almost common sense. And an everyday interpretation of that idea sounds like this: "I'm a good Christian. I don't steal or murder, and I don't even think about committing adultery, at least not too much." We seemingly say to God that we're just fine if we *don't* do certain things.

But listen to the words of Jesus when he was asked by a Sadducee which is the greatest commandment: "Jesus replied: 'Love the Lord your God with all your heart and with all your soul and with all your mind. This is the first and greatest commandment'" (Matthew 22:37-38).

According to Jesus, the goal of a godly life isn't about what you don't do: It's about what you do for God. In a similar way, the goal of parenting is to love your children with all your heart and show that love in concrete ways.

You don't have to be a missionary, pastor, street evangelist, or even a Sunday school teacher to be able to show a passion for God. Teachable moments are an easy yet effective way for you to show your kids that you have a passion for God. Through them your children can see that you love and think about God and are willing to talk about Him. These exposures help ensure they remember that God is a priority in your home.

The positive parenting results of teachable moments are twofold. First, if you want your children to talk about their faith, you must talk about your faith. Eventually, phonies are exposed: Remember Enron, WorldCom, and Adelphia corporations? They could inflate their assets only so long before being caught, and upon examination, the public found out they didn't have anything real to deliver to investors.

Your kids will know if you're really spiritually rich or if you're bankrupt. If you love God, when you use teachable moments, you'll come across as credible, and your children will be much more likely to invest themselves in spiritual matters.

The second positive parenting result from using teachable moments is this: A passion for sharing God is contagious, and your children will catch it.

Have you ever met a person with passion? Young people in love provide a clear example. They think about their boyfriend or girlfriend all day long, perhaps even to distraction. Inevitably, they work information about their girlfriend or boyfriend into every conversation "Oh, so you just got back from India? How interesting. My boyfriend has a jacket that's the color of India ink, but he looks better in blue...." This passion motivates them to rack up phone bills, stay out late, write poetry, sing in the car, or give expensive gifts. In short, they express that passion.

If your passion for God is expressed through teachable moments, the passion to share what God is doing in their lives will also "infect" your children.

The Method

Jesus spent three years with His disciples. He walked with them, taught with them, prayed, fished, and performed miracles with them. They saw Him in action and followed His examples. Throughout the Gospels, Jesus is shown using everyday experiences and events to teach the disciples about God. He often used teachable moments; remember the lessons on salt, light, and the withered tree? Before He died on the cross, Jesus left us with the example for Communion, perhaps the

A Couple of Truths

Children need help to see the long-range consequences of their choices. Teachable moments often encourage kids to choose the godly path in life.

When our daughter Christine was in junior high, we attended a small church, and she was active in the youth group. She had a crush on one boy, but kept it to herself. One by one each of her friends paired up with someone else in the group. I used those couples as an example and shared with Christine my opinion that teens falling in and out of "love" through going together wasn't really going to prepare them for the biblical model of marriage—it more closely resembled divorce. I recommended group activities where Christine could be around her male friends without being pressured to pair up.

After several weeks, Christine mentioned something about a couple that had broken up. When I asked what happened, she told me that all the couples had split up.

"It's not worth it, Mom," she said. "You were right. Dating and going together at this age don't make sense. Besides that, it has ruined a lot of good friendships. I don't want any part of it."

In my spirit I shouted to God, "YES!"

—Jeanne Gowen Dennis

ultimate teachable moment. Setting a pattern through teachable moments is a great way for all parents to teach their children.

Being a leader, especially being a spiritual leader in the home, means that someone is following your example, be it toward heaven or hell. The apostle Paul realized this as a fact of life and boldly encouraged his friends to be like him: "Join with others in following my example, brothers, and take note of those who live according to the pattern we gave you" (Philippians 3:17). He wasn't being boastful; Paul knew by experience that there are measurable, observable, concrete ways to live a godly life.

Raising children to have a strong faith isn't the same as teaching them to walk or talk. Healthy kids would learn those things despite our interference. You need a different method to teach biblical principles. Faith building better resembles the children's game "Simon Says." The leader shows them what to do, and the children follow it. You can pat your head, jump like a bunny, or sing like a bird, and the players will repeat it.

You are the leader in your home. Your children are supposed to follow your example—acting kindly, praying, reading the Bible. Teachable moments provide a perfect way to discuss and play a new game, "God Says."

Teachable moments also allow children to claim the Christian faith as their own. In our culture today, many people pooh-pooh anything that smacks of brainwashing or "forcing your ideas" on someone else. Some parents go so far as to "let children make up their own minds" when it comes to faith issues. They want their children to be unique individuals and, therefore, provide no concrete training. When they are adults, the children are supposed to "choose" which religion they want.

Jeff Leeland describes the dangers of not providing moral and faith guidance to children in his book *Disarming the Teen Heart:*

James was an angry skateboarding teen who grew up in a home where his parents didn't "force" God on him. They never attended church as a family except for weddings or funerals and believed kids should make up their own minds about religion. James grew up calling his mom and dad by their first names. As a 10-year-old, he began smoking pot and drinking at home with the approval of his parents. When he was a child, his first dad would slap him around and intimidate him to keep him in line.

But problems grew in junior high when James's parents divorced. He didn't feel any adult had the right to tell him what to do—especially when he knew they couldn't hit him. He was suspended from school several times for breaking rules, fighting, and verbally attacking his teachers. He feared none of them and resented most of them. He'd fill his time by hanging out at the skate park by day and partying with friends at night. By high school he couldn't handle the "authoritarian" approach of teachers and administrators, so he dropped out. And even though his parents trained him to be a "free thinker," his new step-dad couldn't handle his obnoxious attitude around home and eventually kicked him out.

I (Marianne) was good friends with a neighbor girl, Barbara, when I was in elementary school. I was also emotionally close to her mother. Karen was an intelligent, compassionate woman who had a master's degree in special education and chose to teach in Los Angeles city schools at the poorest of the poor schools. Her philosophy for teaching and parenting revolved around the concept that children are inherently good. Karen believed that if given the proper information, children would choose to do good, and if that didn't work, the consequences of poor choices would shape their destiny in a positive way.

She offered her children no boundaries or discipline or information about God. If Karen's daughter and son wanted to pursue religion, that was fine in her opinion, but they certainly didn't need it.

I remained friends with Barbara through sixth grade. In seventh, we had a parting of the ways when she chose to hang out with the wild crowd. By the end of eighth grade, she was a regular drinker, smoked pot, and had probably already had sex. For my 13th birthday, she gave me a pair of stuffed bears, which I later found out she had shoplifted. She had no curfew, no limits, no parenting.

Her brother, James, who was three years older, was usually getting into trouble as well. He stole my bicycle, hid it, and then tried to light the area on fire when he thought the bike would be discovered. In the seventies he was the first student at our high school to stab another student on campus. I also overheard a conversation between him and Karen in which she explained that pornography was fine but that he would have to decide if he really wanted to be looking at pictures of

It's Not Too Late

Perhaps, for whatever reason, you've never been very intentional about, or personally involved in, your child's spiritual training. Now your child is 16, 17, or 18; busy with school, a job, and friends; pretty set in his ways of thinking and relating to God; and deep into planning for college, a career, or independent living. Haven't you missed your opportunity to be his spiritual mentor? What could you hope to accomplish in the little time you have left with your child at home? The answer is that in only a year, or even just a few months, you can still make an eternal difference. If your teen is beginning his or her senior year of high school, for example, and you start today to use teachable moments, you can share 365 potentially life-changing experiences.

Even if you have only 30 days left before your child goes off to college or joins the military, that's long enough to help him establish the habit of women having sex with dogs. "Do you really think that is natural?" she asked as her way of giving guidance.

Barbara transferred to a nearby high school that offered an alternative program for kids who couldn't cut it in regular classrooms. An intellectually gifted student, Barbara should have excelled, but she couldn't even commit to the watered-down curricula and was on probation. Eventually, her family moved and I lost track of her.

A few years ago, I spoke with Barbara on the phone. Then in her mid-thirties, she was going through an Alcoholics Anonymous program and told me that she was envious of my upbringing—the discipline and religious training my parents had given me. She wished her parents had taught her how to find protection from herself and the strong urges she had toward self-destruction. I told her that God loved her and could help her develop self-control, but her voice was wistful when she said, "Maybe," as though she believed it was really too late.

Using teachable moments to introduce faith allows children to

looking for those ways in which God is revealing Himself. And there's no better habit you could hope to see him take along as he leaves home. It will give him a much better chance of living a morally upright and God-pleasing life. Nor does starting late mean you've got to spend an hour a day feeding the Bible to your teen—we all know that isn't going to happen. Just a few teachable moments a week, wisely and intentionally invested in your child's relationship with the Lord, can plant a love for Him and His Word deep in your teen's heart. Even if your relationship with your teen is rocky, or if it seems awfully late in the game for you to take such an active interest in his or her spiritual life, your sincere desire to have these daily times together gives you a reason to meet and a foundation on which to begin rebuilding the relationship. (In chapter 5, we'll give you ideas on how to construct a great relationship with your child or teen.)

experience faith, not just religion. At some point your children, like James and Barbara, will have to choose their own path, and you want to make sure they know and understand what the Christian path is. A teachable moment offers a chance for a child to absorb a life-changing value, to see God's hand at work, to give him or her a secure foundation. To experience faith is the only way to know faith, and teachable moments offer faith elements that mere Bible memorization doesn't.

Children will each live out the Christian life in a one-of-a-kind way, depending on God's purpose for them and their personality. Only through God can they truly find their unique destiny and purpose. But just as math facts and principles don't change, the priorities and disciplines of leading a spiritual life are the same for each generation. And they must be taught. Teachable moments reveal the patterns of faith living, and if trained by them, your children will have a better chance of recognizing and following those faith patterns when they are adults.

As my (Jim's) children get older, more and more of my teachable moments focus on the way faith is worked out in our lives. Recently, I had the privilege of sharing a special truth with one of my daughters.

"Dad, this isn't how you get to soccer," Joy said, just a trace of panic in her tone. Her coach is firm about the girls being on time to games.

"What do you mean this isn't the way?" I said.

"Well, Mom never goes this way!" was her defense.

"You know, sweetheart," I said, "I think I know how to get where you're supposed to be, and I think I know how to get you there on time."

We stopped at a red light. I could tell she still wasn't convinced. Could that annoying stereotype of the roaming-male-who-won't-ask-for-directions have already infiltrated her 12-year-old mind?

"You may not recognize it," I said, shifting into a teachable-moment gear, "but I know the best way to go and how to do it in the best time.... You know, that's a lot like God. Just as you have to trust me to get you to the right soccer field on time, we have to trust our heavenly Father to get us where we need to go for the purposes He's designed for our lives."

Faith training is also a little like teaching math in the sense that kids need repetition to make the learning stick. Teachers use games, memorization, competitive drills, and tests to teach math. Have you ever noticed that during summer vacations, many kids "forget" their

Rain Thoughts Keep Falling on My Head

There's a drought in our state. Every night, we pray at bedtime for rain. But Justin, age three, doesn't quite have God's involvement with the water cycle all figured out.

"Trees need rain?" he asks in the car.

"Yes," I tell him.

"God makes the rain?" he asks in the bathtub that night, continuing the conversation.

"Yes," I tell him.

"My sister needs rain?" he asks at the park three days later.

"Yes."

"Cows need rain?" he asks at the dinner table one night.

"Yes."

"No they not," he says. "They need milk."

I can't persuade him that cows drink water and produce milk, but that's not really the issue. As Justin figures out rain and the other complex things of life, it's paramount that I be there when he has these questions, to be part of the ongoing conversation about life, to offer information from a biblical perspective. I have to be available to him when he needs to talk, because the questions—and answers—are only going to get tougher.

—mkh

math? Ask them in July what seven times eight equals, and they'll give you a look as blank as a new sheet of paper. If kids are to remember their faith lessons, those principles must be reinforced from time to time. Teachable moments offer parents a perfect way to introduce gentle faith-building reminders.

In February 2002, Federal Reserve Chairman Alan Greenspan commented that a good foundation in math would improve financial literacy and "help prevent younger people from making poor financial decisions that can take years to overcome." In the same way, if parents make the effort to use teachable moments to explain the basics about "spiritual literacy," that effort may keep your children from making poor spiritual decisions that can take years to overcome.

CHAPTER FOUR

How to Teach Without Preaching

We all know them. Those people who teach us about life just by being who they are. The ones who make an indelible mark on our lives by saying nothing yet doing something extraordinary. They lead by example and teach by their lifestyle.

They are the grandfather who never complained even when faced with death by emphysema, struggling for every breath; the teacher who was passionate about history and gave you that same love for people dead well over a thousand years; the physically challenged sixth-grader who went out for the track team and never placed in a race, never came in anything except last, and yet when he finished the season drew more applause than the record-breaking sprinters. They are that special aunt who woke you up with hymns every morning played on the piano and somehow transferred her joy of worship to you; the high school homecoming queen who took a boy with Down syndrome to the prom.

For my (Jim's) family, one of those people is Terri. She has cancer, and never once have we seen her faith falter. She doesn't ask, "Why me?" or get angry with God. The pain she's gone through is horrendous, but her countenance reflects peace and hope. I tell my children often to think of her, to remember what gut-level faith looks like in the face of physical decay, something we'll all face in one way or another. Terri is our example, one of those people who has taught us the mysteries of faith without saying a word.

A good parent also sets an example to live by. This is modeling, and it's one of the most profound ways you can influence your kids. Even if you don't yet have a mighty faith, you can teach simple, basic spiritual lessons. If you pray every evening before dinner, for example, it doesn't take long for your children to acquire the same habit.

Carrie Johnson, a college student at Biola University, learned about worship from watching her parents. Her father, Chuck Johnson, the editorial director for Focus on the Family's different magazines, shares this anecdote:

Monkey See, Monkey Do

Whenever three-year-old Justin wants to play a computer game, he finds the CD-ROM and gives it to his twin brother, Kendrick. Kendrick then opens the drive, puts in the disc, clicks through the "my computer" and "drive D" icons until the game is opened. He has even successfully loaded a computer game all by himself. I once found him frustrated that he couldn't reconfigure the display settings to successfully play an older game.

I never taught him to do this on his own; in fact, the twins aren't allowed to play on the computer without supervision. He learned, nevertheless, by watching me. He soaked it all in with his eyes, and when given the chance, he repeated what he saw. All things considered, CD-ROM loading is a good skill to learn.

Kendrick also picks up bad skills in the same way. One day my husband

> When Carrie was about four, my wife, Gwen, and I had been married a little over 10 years, and the church asked us to sponsor the engaged-and-newlywed class at church. We would have Bible studies at our house one evening a week, and Carrie would inevitably creep out and sit on the stairway to listen to the singing led by one of the men. One time we were singing "I've Got a River of Life," and she came down to join us. She crouched down in the middle of the room, and then jumping as high as she could, she'd belt out the chorus, "Spring up, O well, within my soul!" She says a lot of her love for worship and music started during those evenings—and of course the young couples thought she was absolutely adorable.

Children will pick up character traits like diligence, compassion, and honesty in the same way. If you act virtuously, they will see that

fixed the toilet. Kendrick watched him try to unclog the line by donning latex gloves and using his hands. Now at least once a day, I catch Kendrick shoving things down the toilet, and most of the time it's his arm. Fortunately, he has also learned to flush first.

Kendrick is also the one who imitates compassion. If I fall down, he is the one who helps me up and kisses the "owie." For all his quietness, when Kendrick does speak, he tries to repeat the phrases and intonations he has heard. When he's angry, he'll put his hands on his hips, look you in the eye, and say, "You're not hearing to me!"

For good or bad, Kendrick will be our son who is most likely to be "monkey see, monkey do." It's up to me to make sure the things he sees are godly and the things he hears are worth repeating.

—mkh

and take note. But you need to go one step farther to make sure the lesson hits home.

Here's how it works: One day I (Jim) found a billfold in a hotel parking lot. It had money in it but no identification. I took it to the front desk, placed it on the counter, and told the hotel clerk, "In case someone comes looking for a wallet, here it is."

My children witnessed the event, and I could have left the matter there, but I chose not to. Instead we discussed the virtue of honesty and why I turned in the money instead of keeping it. I wasn't trying to impress them with my virtue; I was impressing on them biblical truths. Perhaps they would have learned the lesson just by watching,

A Gift Horse

Through countless teachable moments, I've taught my 15-year-old-daughter, Lauren, that she needs to be patient and learn to wait on the Lord for His timing. Throughout her life, I've seen her develop a trust in God that is beyond her years.

Ever since she was five, my daughter has been captivated by horses. When she was nine, Lauren began working year-round cleaning stables to earn money for riding lessons. She performed this miserable work diligently and learned to ride, but we still couldn't afford to buy her a horse.

Recently, my mother offered to buy her one. Lauren's dream was to own a Hanoverian, which was out of the price range and, therefore, out of the question. As we began looking for the "perfect" horse, we stumbled upon a reasonably priced thoroughbred. Had God dropped the perfect horse right into Lauren's lap? It was too good to be true. All that was left was the health checkup.

While Lauren was away at camp, the trainer and I discovered that the perfect horse was a perfect wreck. The sellers had tried to mask a severe but I couldn't be sure without asking them what they were thinking. By passing up the money, I was able to invest in my children's spiritual education, and I know teachable moments like that will pay off in an "honest-to-goodness" future.

Note: I wasn't preaching. No one got a lecture; no one left feeling inadequate, overwhelmed, or bored. It took a couple of minutes, but I did intentionally teach them the principle "Each of you should look not only to your own interests, but also to the interests of others" (Philippians 2:4).

Parents can deliberately and intentionally teach their children biblical truths—and the children can enjoy it. It's not some fanciful

allergy with steroids. I said to the trainer, "Find me another horse in our price range by Friday!" She laughed. I cried all the way home.

When I told Lauren by phone, she calmly said, "It's okay, Mom. I'm disappointed, but I know that God knows what He's doing. He knows I couldn't go through watching a horse be so ill. He has something better for me. I'd rather not have a horse if it's not all right with God."

Next day the trainer called. "You're never going to believe what I'm standing here looking at!" she said. "A perfectly healthy three-year-old Hanoverian mare, imported from Germany. Her father was the Grand Prix winner. And...the owner's willing to drop the price."

On Friday, we surprised Lauren with the horse God wanted her to have. When she saw Dona Hella, Lauren threw her arms around me and sobbed with joy. The joy represented more than having a horse, the fulfillment of her dreams. The joy also sprang from trusting God to provide at the right time and place. By placing her dream in God's hands, she allowed Him to provide the best. This teachable moment lasted more than nine years, but it was worth every second of the wait.

—Kalie Lasley

dream or nebulous ideal you hear about only on the *700 Club*. And you don't have to be a natural-born teacher to use the principles outlined in this chapter. You just have to try them out and work with them for a few weeks, and soon you'll know the secrets of teaching without preaching.

Let the Situation Teach

James Werning, a Focus on the Family employee for 13 years and a father of four, recalls this defining moment:

> Over the years, my wife, Joan, and I have welcomed several unwed mothers into our home. Our four children watch and listen as we provide a loving place for these women (girls, really) while they deal with the stress of pregnancy and learn to manage their lives.
>
> One of those women was named Darlene, and she was the catalyst for one of our most memorable teachable moments. On this particular occasion, Darlene had had a horrendous day trying to take her newborn to doctor visits, schedule daycare, go to work, get car repairs—everything mothers (and fathers) do. At the dinner table that night, her frustration let loose in a sermon aimed especially at our three girls, then ages 11, nine, and six.
>
> "Don't do what I did, okay?" Darlene said, tapping the table in emphasis. "Get married first. Then have babies. Not the other way around."
>
> It was just that simple. Her passion and vehemence made an impression on my girls they still remember, even three years later.

While Darlene didn't go into the spiritual reasons for keeping baby-making activities confined to marriage, her message gave the Wernings the perfect reason to follow up with a Bible study or short discussion about what the Bible says about sex and marriage. What Darlene gave them was a touch of reality to spark the conversation—proof that God's standards are for our benefit and that if we flout them, there will be a price to pay.

Like the billfold, Darlene's speech was a memorable catalyst for a short lesson on a life principle. If you keep your discussions focused on the catalyst or situation, no one is threatened or feels like a lecture is coming on.

Here's another example.

Picture my (Jim's) entire family on a train from Paris to Versailles. We rode, and rode, and rode, and at last, very late at night, we arrived at the station. Everybody else got off—and still we sat, because the train had stopped, but not in Versailles. Finally, we realized the train was at the end of the line and we had no idea where we were or where to go. The only thing we could do was step out onto the platform.

Everyone was gone, and then this woman came from nowhere. I said, "Excuse me," introduced myself, and shared my family's plight. She responded in English! She was able to tell us where we should have switched trains, and a few minutes later she came back with a train schedule written in English.

Later on, my wife, Janet, and I were able to remind the kids through a teachable moment that God takes care of the details because He cares. He provided a kind translator for us when were lost in Europe, and He'll take care of the other little things in our lives as well. Through God's intervention, we got the kids on the right train as well as the right train of thought—all that without a lecture, raised voice, or boring sermon.

The Right Time and the Right Place

What if the catalyst is your child's awful behavior? Yes, please discipline. Impose a consequence or send the child to his or her room until things settle down. No, please don't preach or teach or lecture or even discuss things when either you or your child is angry. This leads nowhere because your child isn't ready to listen, so save your breath.

If you're angry, go for a walk, take a shower, or do something to take your mind off it and relax. This will save you from giving a fine lecture that will fall on deaf ears. By setting up the consequences before an infraction takes place, there is no arguing, and usually a lesson is learned.

I (Jim) recall a particular evening when I was a teenager. I got a call from a friend who wanted to double date and go see *Easy Rider* at a drive-in theater. I wasn't allowed to go to a drive-in with a girl, because the privacy of a car could lead to physical passion. I also wasn't allowed to see R-rated movies, and *Easy Rider* was R-R-Revving in sex and violence. My father had earlier set up the consequences. Breaking either of the two rules would lead to being grounded for a week. I decided to go with my friends anyway.

After the movie, my pals dropped me off at home first so I could at least make my curfew. That was the only break I got that night. As I was creeping up the stairs, trying not to be heard, my father greeted me. "Hi, Jim, did you have a good evening?"

Without looking him in the eye, I said, "Yeah, Dad, but I'm tired. I'm going to bed."

Ignoring my comment, he said, "Where did you go on your date?"

"A movie, Dad. Goodnight."

"Let me ask you this: Did the movie theater have a roof on top?"

"Uh, well, no, Dad, it didn't."

"You're grounded one week," he said as a matter of fact.

"Okay, Dad. 'Night."

"One more thing—what was the movie rated?"

I climbed two more stairs. "Uh, well, it was rated R."

"That's two weeks you're grounded."

"Goodnight, Dad."

"Goodnight, Jim."

There was no discussion because there was nothing to discuss. I knew the rules, and I broke them. The consequences were in place, so we didn't have an argument.

Preparing in advance for large life lessons is also a great way to teach without preaching. I try to reinforce the lessons that God gives my children so they remember them. Consider Joshua's college career. He's not your average kid. He excels at public speaking; at 20, he's an accomplished evangelist. But he didn't excel in high school academics. He graduated with a 2.1 grade point average and, as a result, decided to enroll in an Internet distance-learning program through Liberty University. That way he could live at home, be free to evangelize, and also improve his scholastic record.

Then through a wonderfully orchestrated series of events, Joshua was offered a chance to attend Moody Bible Institute in Chicago. That was a dream come true for a kid like Joshua. His interests and talents matched Moody's curriculum. But Joshua's transcript didn't match Moody's requirements; the average student at Moody has a GPA of 3.8. There was no earthly reason for Joshua to be accepted into that caliber of school. But there was a heavenly reason: God wanted him there.

Josh and I talk about this a lot—sort of like a teachable moment miniseries. We discuss that when God has a plan for your life, it doesn't matter what the obstacles are. God will clear all those obstacles for you, just as he did for Joshua at Moody. We saw the hand of God move those obstacles and position Josh in the place he needs to be. It's kind of like his personal parting of the Red Sea, and I don't want him to forget it.

Because Josh and I talk about this in a positive, everyday, casual way, I probably won't ever be tempted to give him a long sermon about God's providence. We tackle those big lessons day by day, conversation by conversation.

Less Is More

When it comes to teachable moments, less on the subject means that more is remembered, and retention is the key. In this way you avoid giving your kids too much information and hearing the dreaded words *That's boring*.

My (Marianne's) daughter, Danielle, loves to watch *Antiques Road Show*, and I confess there's a certain suspense when someone brings in, say, an old German porcelain doll and the appraiser's eyes bulge when he recognizes the signature mark left by the manufacturer. Then he calmly describes the condition of the doll, gives the history, compliments the lace dress and then—the moment we've been waiting for—declares the value!

Sometimes it's in the thousands; sometimes it's as low as $25. But whatever the price estimate, it is satisfying to have a concrete answer, an end to the suspense.

One night after watching the program, I was just about to send Danielle to brush her teeth. Just then a truth hit me. "Hey," I said, "if you were on *Antiques Road Show* and Jesus were the appraiser, how much would he say you're worth?"

Her face flashed a smile of happiness and confidence. "I'm priceless!"

An easy question with no real suspense, no surprise. But I couldn't resist using the moment to remind her in a unique way that Jesus cherishes her.

Go with God's Flow

When your children are in a learning situation, sit back and let their life circumstances do the teaching, and you do the clapping from the sidelines.

After 17 years of employment with the same company, Ray F. was laid off. With no job prospects in sight, he had to budget his savings, and his three older children would have to alter their lifestyle. They would have to use their own money for things that he and his wife, Jean, had previously paid for. Here's more of his story:

> I watched as my kids struggled with wanting to buy a 50-cent can of pop out of a machine when they knew if they waited they could buy a whole liter for a dollar. Then if they waited, they sometimes realized they could do without the soda altogether. We also volunteer regularly to help feed the homeless at the local Red Cross shelter. We cook the meals and take them to the shelter. On one occasion we saw a family from our church living there. Through these experiences, my kids have learned not to take things for granted and to thank God for what He has provided through this trial. There's no way I could have taught them the lessons they learned from those life experiences. They can now tell the difference between necessities and desires, the value and the non-value of certain items, and they have observed many answered prayers.
>
> I've seen our 13-year-old, Michael, mature. He earned $60 helping a neighbor paint his house, and the first thing Michael did was donate 10 percent to the church. I was impressed that he would do that, considering he was also paying for his activities and treats on his own.

Now that Ray has a new job, he says, "The hard part will be sustaining all the lessons we learned." Will it be so difficult? Or will it be easier now than before the children experienced the trials? The last few months brought Ray's family a smorgasbord of topics to talk about and use as a reference point for future discussions. If Ray and Jean capture those lessons and turn them into teachable moments, they can reinforce what God has taught their children. Ray and Jean can affirm and articulate the solid life lessons their children learned by merely reminding them of what God did. No muss, no fuss, no bothersome preaching.

Teaching Deliberately

Working God and biblical truths into everyday conversations doesn't require three points and fist banging; you don't even need to shake a pointed finger. Beth Weeden recalls a time when she impressed her son, then a fifth-grader, with a truth about commitment:

To Complain or Not to Complain?

Mr. X is one of those maverick teachers who doesn't really care what people think about him. I had him for a history/social studies class my sophomore year in high school.

One Friday afternoon, Mr. X lectured about the birth of Christianity, derived from form and source criticism, which analyzes biblical writings in light of other ancient literary works and oral traditions. This method of analysis can lead one to believe that the biblical account is not accurate. I didn't agree with many of his conclusions. During class, some of my Christian classmates were getting upset, almost crying, but I was silent.

On the way to a band performance the next day, some of my friends from class asked why I hadn't said anything to defend my faith. (On other occasions I had been quite vocal.) I told them that I hadn't been prepared with solid arguments, and I didn't feel like making a fool of myself.

On Sunday, I talked with my parents. They encouraged me to prepare my arguments rationally and conclusively. They didn't want Mr. X to look down on me because I was young, and they wanted me to set a good example;

I was heavily involved with PTO. As vice president of fund-raising, I regretted the commitment as the end-of-the-year activities piled up. I was just too busy. Seeing my frustration, Matt asked, "Can't you just quit?"

I explained, "When you make a commitment, you have to carry it through, even though you may want to stop."

Through that moment and others, Matt learned how to follow through with his commitments. In his senior year of high school, he had significant roles in two theater productions, *Fiddler on the Roof* and *Up the Down Staircase*. By the spring of that year, he felt like quitting drama because of the

basically, that's what the Bible says to do in 1 Timothy 4:12: "Don't let anyone look down on you because you are young, but set an example for the believers in speech, in life, in love, in faith and in purity."

I spent six hours on Sunday preparing a PowerPoint presentation with 20 slides. I addressed the two issues of form and source criticism and explained a more conservative way to approach biblical texts.

While I was doing this, other parents were trying to get Mr. X into hot water by complaining about him to the principal.

On Monday, I told Mr. X that I had some problems with the issues he had brought up on Friday. I gave him a transcript of my presentation so he could preview it, and then I asked him if I could have class time to present it. He said yes and even helped to get a projector. He gave me the whole class period, and we remained friends.

Through this event, my parents helped me learn how to disagree without being disagreeable; I found that it took a lot more work than complaining, which wouldn't have had any effect on a tough teacher like Mr. X anyway. In the long run, the preparation was well worth it.

—Peter Sidebotham

demanding schedule and the emotional energy required to get along with the rest of the cast. But he stuck with it, and at the final performance, my husband and I applauded not only his great acting ability but also his self-discipline.

Parents can have an even more structured agenda and still keep the attention of their children with a good object lesson. Albert Yeh tells about a lesson he taught his children while preparing for baseball season:

> We purchased my 11-year-old son, Kyle, a new glove. On a warm Sunday afternoon, Kyle, my five-year-old daughter, Moriah, and I worked together to rub oil into the leather to break in the new glove. Both kids were amazed to see how the glove began to soften with each oil-heat application and how much easier it was to form the glove to the shape of the owner's hand. After the treatment, it was much easier to catch a ball.
>
> I told the kids that a new glove is hard and stubborn. Even though the gloves are designed to catch a baseball, it often seems as if the glove wants to work against us by not bending the way we want it to. This makes it difficult for the glove to do its job.
>
> Christians are just like a new glove. God had a purpose in mind when He designed each person, but just like a glove that hasn't been broken in, we often fight against His will. Only through yielding to His warm love do we begin to take shape in the way He wants us, and by conforming to God's hand, we will be able to serve Him most effectively.

Make Teaching Fun

My (Marianne's) daughter, Danielle, is usually well-behaved. But every once in a while she has her moments. One day we were shopping for school supplies before having our planned date. In the car, she started to beg and whine for something, a behavior that I absolutely do not tolerate. When I pointed that out, she wilted, saying, "I've lost my privilege for the date, haven't I?"

With a rare burst of wisdom I said, "No. You'll never lose your date times. Dates aren't a reward for good or bad behavior; we have dates because you're my daughter, and I need to be with you. I will always love you, no matter what you do. Also, God would never turn away from me if I wanted to be close to Him. I want to love you in the same way God loves me."

That set the date times apart from privileges, which can be taken away as a consequence. She gets dates because of her position as my child, not as a result of her abilities or actions. Because of the security and trust that dates represent to Danielle, the times are even dearer than ever. We recently watched an action video at home together as a date, and in that cozy, informal atmosphere we discussed the themes in the movie: justice, revenge, doing one's duty, the changes of adolescence, and using your gifts for the benefit of others. The conversations occurred naturally and at Danielle's prompting. In a warm, fun atmosphere, she's more likely to ask questions and be receptive to my answers.

If you do have a formal teaching episode, add a little fun. Here are two examples the Weidmanns have used to teach their children a specific truth in a fun, unforgettable way:

1. Jim asked his children to stand side by side as he placed a water balloon between their shoulders. He then asked them to carry the balloon a certain distance using only the pressure of their shoulders—no hands. When they had finished and the inevitable water fight had ended, he was able to teach them the concept based on Matthew 11:27-30—when you are yoked with God, you see what He sees, you feel what He feels.

2. Jim brought the kids in one by one, blindfolded, and asked them to hold out their hands as he placed an object in them. It was

cold, slimy, and had a strange texture. "What do you think is the most powerful thing on earth?" he asked. "A bomb" was the common answer. "No," he said. "It's this. What you are touching is so powerful that only God can control it. What is it?" The children were holding an entire three-pound cow tongue (you can find one in the frozen food section), and he used it to teach the lesson from James 3:8 that the tongue is uncontrollable except with help from the Holy Spirit.

Questions Are Better Than Answers

Sometimes asking your kids questions is better than giving them answers.

"Jesus died on the cross like Frogger died in the water?" Justin, almost four, asked. He was trying to make sense of a video game where the main character, a frog, has five lives each session.

"Yes," I (Marianne) said hesitantly.

"Don't worry," he said. "Jesus will come back just like Frogger."

"Is Frogger real?" I asked.

"Yes."

"Is Jesus real?" I asked.

"Yes."

I then tried to explain the difference between Jesus, whom Justin has never seen, and the very visual Frogger, whom he sees too much of.

By asking our kids questions, we can find out about them and what they need to know. Using questions instead of lectures to teach our children accomplishes three things:

1. It builds the relationship.
2. It starts a conversation.
3. It keeps the information specific to what your kids need to know at that precise moment.

If you want to start a conversation with your kids, here are some topics and suggested questions to get their tongues wagging. (The questions are geared for middle school kids on up. For younger children, rephrase the questions in a way they can understand and be selective about the topics.)

School

- Did anyone tell a good joke today? What was it about?
- Was the teacher in a good mood? How could you tell?
- What is your teacher like when he or she is in a bad mood?
- What is the best thing your teacher does?
- What don't you like about your teacher?
- How does your teacher keep the class under control? Is it effective? What could he or she do differently? What would you do differently?
- If you were the teacher, how would you have run this class?
- Whom did you talk to today? What about?
- If Jesus were the principal at your school, what would He do?
- What was special about this school day that made it different from all the others?
- What could you have done today to make the day different for someone else?
- If you could get a nickel for every time you heard someone say something nice or a nickel for every time someone said something mean, which would you choose? How long would it take you to earn $100?
- What do you do best at in school? How can you tell?
- What does it feel like to do something you like and to do a good job at it?
- If you could do anything you wanted at lunch, what would it be?
- Which one of the adults at your school is the kindest? What does he or she do that you like? How can you be more like that person?
- If you were the principal for a day, what would you do?
- How does school help you fulfill your dreams?

The Media

- What is it about this form of entertainment that attracts you? Why do you like this particular style (or genre or show) more than others?
- Why do you listen to or watch that? (If it's simply because friends do, ask, "Why do your friends listen to or watch it?")
- How does this form of entertainment make you feel?
- Do the themes reflect reality? Do they reflect truth? If they reflect reality, do they also gloss over evil?
- How do the messages conveyed compare with the values you've been taught here at home or in church?
- Do you think these messages have any effect on how close you feel to your family, friends, or God? Why or why not?
- Would you feel comfortable if Jesus sat here listening to or watching this with you? Do you think He'd be concerned, or would He enjoy this particular entertainment product?
- Does this entertainment reflect an opinion about God? What is it?
- What would happen if you imitated the lifestyles and choices of the characters in these songs or this program?
- What do you consider to be inappropriate entertainment? Where do you draw the line? Where does Scripture draw the line? Are they the same?
- How does it make you feel to know that by purchasing a CD, going to a movie, or watching a TV show, you are supporting the ideas being promoted?

Friends

- Which student/friend is the kindest in your class or group of friends? What does he or she do that you like? Why do you want to be that person's friend?
- Who is the least popular kid at school? What does that kid feel like when he or she is at school?

- How do you treat that kid? How would Jesus treat that kid?
- If something really embarrassing happened to you, which one of your friends would be least likely to tell your secret? How do you know?
- If you all went to the mall together, which one of your friends might ask you to shoplift? Which one would be most likely to say, "That's wrong"?
- Who is the person at school least likely to get in a fight? Why did you choose that person? Would you like to be more like that person?
- Who are the Christians in your class? How can you tell?

Choice Words

"Are we like puppets to God?" Isaac asked me on Monday.

"No. Why do you ask?"

He didn't answer.

I took a finger puppet and put it on. "See? The puppet has to do whatever I make it do."

Then I put the puppet on his finger, explaining that the puppet either had to love him if he made it, or it could choose to love him or not. "Which do you like better? If the puppet has to love you, or if it can choose?"

"Has to."

Hmmm. I decided I needed to offer a different perspective. I picked Isaac up and held him tight.

"Now, you have to love me. You have to, have to, have to," I said.

He squirmed and wanted down. I set him on his feet and said, "Now, if you'd like to—you don't have to if you don't want—but if you want to give me one, I'd really like a hug." He grinned and hugged me. Then he said, "I choose to love God" and went skipping off.

—Katherine Grace Bond

- Where do you eat lunch? Who sits with you?
- Who are the three most important people to you? Did you talk to them today? What about?
- Who is the most unhappy person in your class or among your friends? How do you know? What can you do for that person?
- Which one of your friends will give you the best advice? Why did you choose that person? Would the advice be based on the Bible? If not, what would it be based on?
- What are your standards for choosing friends? Which of your friends comes closest to that standard? Which one is farthest from that standard?
- Do you want more friends? Why?
- What does it feel like when a friend lets you down? Will Jesus ever let you down?

Family

- If you had a million dollars to spend on a family vacation, where would you go and what would you do?
- If you were to design a new house for the family, how would you draw it? (Or ask them to draw the house.)
- If Jesus were your brother, how would He treat you?
- If Jesus were you, how would He treat (name of sibling)?
- What's one thing you can do to treat (name of sibling) as Jesus would?
- If you were in charge of teaching the Bible at this house, what would you do?
- Do you sometimes feel like everyone is too busy for you? Tell me about that feeling.
- What are you looking forward to most this weekend with the family?
- What is your least favorite family activity?

- Are you happier at home or at school (or church or soccer practice; you get the idea)? Why?
- Tell me about a time when I did something you really liked. What did that feel like?

Hobbies

- What do you like about your hobby? How does it make you feel when you are pursuing your hobby?
- If you could spend time on your hobby or go to church, which one would you pick? Why?
- If Jesus participated in your hobby, would He do it differently? How would He use the hobby to help others? How can you use your hobby to help others?
- Is there a way to make money from your hobby? Would that make it more fun? Why or why not?
- Do you have plans for your hobby? What are they? How can I help?
- Do you spend enough time on your hobby? How much time would be enough? How much time would be too much? How do you make those decisions?

Church

- If you had your choice between your favorite movie or going to church, which one would you choose? Why?
- Tell me about a good time you had at church. How did you feel?
- Tell me about a bad time at church. How did you feel?
- Does your Sunday school teacher or youth group leader love God? How can you tell?
- If your Sunday school teacher or youth group leader is in a bad mood, how can you tell? How does it make you feel?
- If Jesus ran your Sunday school class or youth group, what would He do differently? What would He do the same?

- What could you do to make church more interesting so that you would invite your friends?
- What about our church would appeal to your friends? What wouldn't?
- Do your church friends love God? How can you tell?
- Do you like your church friends or your school friends better? Why?
- When you grow up, what would you like to do at church? What sounds fun?

What's Your Line?

One day Janae was invited to see a movie with two of her friends. I dropped her off at the movie theater and continued on to the car repair shop to complete an errand. While I was there, my cell phone rang. I answered; it was Janae.

"Hi, Dad," she said. "I need you to come pick me up."

I glanced at my watch. "Sweetheart, where are you?" I asked, confused.

"I'm still at the movie, Dad. I walked out early."

"Why did you do that?"

"They used God's name in vain in the movie."

She paused while I thought back to the conversation we had just had weeks before. We had discussed choosing the line where an action dishonors God.... Specifically we had discussed movies, videos, and television. I had said that using God's name in vain was my line. If I heard it, I left the movie. And now my daughter had done the same thing.

"Uh, Dad," she said, her voice quiet, "I want to let you know that I feel real bad, because they had to use it twice before I walked out."

I chuckled. "Oh, sweetheart," I reassured her, "God's smiling because you're getting the message."

—J.W.

- If Jesus moved to our city, would He attend our church? Why or why not?
- Do the people at our church love God? How can you tell?

The Best Example

If you really want to teach your kids to be connected with God without preaching at them, you have to get them to see that God is relevant to their lives and that they have a purpose in His plans. That'll charge them up like nothing else, and they will learn more through that experience than through any other teaching method.

I (Jim) always encourage my kids that if they live out their faith, God will reward them with joy. Here's an example: A while back I had become a bit preoccupied with Janae's homecoming dance. I was beginning to realize what dating was like from a girl's perspective. The way I figured it, the guy was always in control; he could either ask or not ask, but at least he had the option. Girls wait. And then wait some more. They don't have an option if no one asks them. They're constantly wondering if they're good enough, if anyone will notice them, if anyone will ask the important question.

Janae called me at work one day, and her voice was bubbling over with joy. "Dad, I gotta tell you something!" she said.

I bet she got asked to homecoming. Some guy figured out what a great kid she is! I almost said something about the dance, but instead I blurted, "Tell me!"

"A girl came up to me in class, and she said, 'Why are you always so happy?' and I said, 'It's because I have a personal relationship with Jesus Christ,' and she said, 'I think I need one too.'"

Someone had noticed Janae. Someone had asked the important question.

Janae was more thrilled that she had a purpose and a partnership in God's kingdom than she would be if a thousand guys asked her to the dance. She learned more in that moment about being in God's will than from any family night or teachable moment I have ever presented. And now, she's an example to others; she's teaching without preaching at her school.

CHAPTER FIVE

A Good Relationship: The First Component of a Teachable Moment

The first and most significant component of a successful teachable moment is a good parent-child relationship. We've already seen that kids and teens desire time with their parents and that time spent with our children produces an opportunity to use teachable moments. Relationship is what creates the atmosphere so that teachable moments yield spiritual fruit.

The correlation between relationships and using teachable moments can be illustrated by the success of the Kellogg brothers in 1894. Their primary goal was to create a new kind of cracker-like granola bar from corn. After preparing a mixture, they rolled it out and left it to dry; when they returned to the kitchen, they found the mixture stale. Not wanting to waste the food, the brothers forced it between the rollers anyway in an attempt to make a long sheet of dough. The dried mixture broke into flakes. Thus, the first breakfast cereal was born.

After working diligently on one goal, the Kellogg brothers transformed the basic ingredient of corn into a new product that changed the way Americans think about breakfast.

If parents work diligently on building a relationship with their children, they will almost assuredly find the basic ingredients of a good relationship transform into something spiritually greater. Teachable moments can create a new product, spiritual awareness, that changes the way your children think about God.

Your relationship with your child is the basis of any successful teaching; respect, obedience, and spiritual training all occur in the context of relationship. That's why Ephesians 6:4 says, "Fathers, do not exasperate your children; instead bring them up in the training and instruction of the Lord."

To give you an example of how key relationship is to spiritual mentoring, read this brief scenario and answer the question at the end.

You're in the minivan on the way to violin lessons. The preschoolers are asleep in their car seats. You hear a small voice from the very back say something, but you couldn't make out the words. You turn off the radio.

"What is it?" you say, half turning, half keeping your eye on the road.

"Nobody in orchestra likes Alison anymore," your child says. "She's bossy now that she's first chair."

You respond:

a. *"Well, just stay out of her way then."*
b. *"I've been in situations like that before. Would you like to tell me what happened in orchestra today?"*
c. *"Listen, Alison is your leader now. The Bible says you have to 'obey the rulers.' So be humble and get over it."*
d. *"Honey, please be quiet. I'm trying to drive."*

If you responded anything except *b*, you missed an opportunity to improve your relationship with your child and to take advantage of a teachable moment. All the other responses shut down the conversation and thereby ruin any opportunity for you to find out what is going on in your child's heart.

Answer *a* gives your child a solution to the problem, but she won't learn anything about relationships and forgiveness. It also does not help the child think through her options and choose the most biblical response.

Answer *c* is preachy, and it may or may not address the real issue behind the statement your child made. What if your child is wondering

Teachable Moments Remembered #2

- "We had devotions as a family. My dad would read from the Character Sketch book, which tells stories about animals and how they display different qualities we all should emulate. Also, my dad and mom were always open and willing to have deep spiritual conversation with me. They wanted to know what God was teaching me."
- "My dad rotated among us kids, taking us out for breakfast Saturday mornings. We would talk about what was going on in our lives. We would also all talk after Sunday lunch about our spiritual lives and where we were at."
- "My father took me to a father/daughter camp in California for a week. Our time together was special, and our relationship was strengthened. We also both grew spiritually during this time and helped to keep each other accountable."
- "From the time I was in fourth or fifth grade until I was in high school, Dad and I would get up at 6 a.m. and read to each other [books with biblical themes]. These special times taught me how important a daily time with the Lord is. I will always treasure them because they belonged only to Dad and me—no one else. I had his undivided attention."
- "In eighth grade, I was really struggling with knowing that God was knocking at the door of my heart, but I didn't know what to do with that. Mom took me into her bedroom and led me in a prayer asking Christ to come into my life."

how to encourage Alison? What if your child wants to quit orchestra? What if your child wants to try to advance to first chair himself? Answer *c* may be part of the answer, but it is given in such a way that limits further discussion and makes it difficult for your child to receive willingly.

Answer *d* indirectly tells your child that she's not important, and that may hinder your relationship from developing. You've lost a moment you may never recapture. If you really can't drive and talk at the same time, a better answer would be, "It sounds like you've got something on your mind. It's very important to me to listen, but right now I need to concentrate on driving. Can we talk about it right after violin lesson?"

Answer *b* tells your child that you are interested in her thoughts and problems and that you've had a similar experience. It lets her know that you care about what is going on in orchestra and can empathize

Battle of the Boots

One of the best pieces of parenting advice I ever received was to "choose my battles." No one has the emotional energy to fight children over every little thing, so wise parents save their reserves for the big battles that could have eternal consequences. For example, I do not choose my daughter's clothes. As long as they are modest and appropriate for the occasion, she may wear whatever colors or styles she wants (and we can afford). She's in a tomboy stage now, and so we shop in the boys' department. That's fine with me because the shorts are long and the shirts are loose. There is no gender identity problem because of her delicate build and her long, bouncy ponytail. If you ask Danielle, she'll tell you that my relaxed attitude toward clothes is one of the things she appreciates about me the most. It's done wonders to keep our relationship smooth during her middle school years.

When I had the twins, I didn't think I'd have clothing issues with them with her emotional pain. It also gives you a chance to find out what lesson, if any, your child is ready to learn. Answer *b* reflects that you are interested in a relationship, an exchange of ideas, getting to know your child, and that you are willing to talk about yourself. It is the answer that says the parent-child relationship is first, the learning second.

How Do Good Relationships Affect Teachable Moments?

Relationship Rule Number One: Building common interests creates opportunities for teachable moments.

My (Marianne's) daughter, Danielle, doesn't have a passion for my hobbies; she doesn't want to develop a discipline for music, she won't play chess for long, and softball isn't a hit with her. But we do like to

until they were teens. And then Kendrick turned two and fell in love with his bright red rain boots. If I left his bedroom closet open and he saw them, he squished his feet into them and wouldn't take them off without a fight. He wore them in all seasons, to any event. At first I tried to make him change when we left the house, but the fighting wasn't worth it. Sure he looked a little silly, and the plastic made his feet smell like overripe onions, but there was nothing morally wrong with the boots, so I gave in.

I'm glad I decided to surrender. Those boots meant so much to him. He beamed when he wore them; he was proud. Most of the stares he received were friendly ones, and I once overheard a child compliment me: "I can't believe he gets to wear those boots to church. His mom is nice."

I ask myself, In 10 years, will it matter that he wore the boots to church? And I answer, Yes. He'll know that relationships are more important than shoes.

—mkh

play cards and read the same books. What do you and your child do together that you both enjoy?

These activities don't have to be expensive, overly time-consuming or intellectually demanding. Throw a baseball, play Monopoly, or share a subscription to a cooking magazine. If you can't think of at least three things, ask your child what he or she wants to do, and try new things until you hit on an interest you can share.

Once you have interests in common to discuss, you'll be able to broaden the conversation to other topics, including spiritual things. Teachable moments will begin to take shape naturally and strengthen your parent-child bond. Caring about his special interests lets your child know you have a special interest in him.

Kari Krager tells about the time she discovered a teachable moment when she took an interest in her son's passion for ancient Egypt. Here's "The Pyramid Scam":

> A documentary about ancient Egypt and the pyramids was on. My seven-year-old son and I sat enraptured as the host explained the history of the pyramids; soon he was talking about the Tower of Babel and showing a close-up of some text from Genesis. Parts of the "history" sounded strange to me, and after the show was over I grabbed two Bibles. Perry and I read Genesis 11 from both versions out loud and discovered that the host hadn't been entirely truthful. The show had mixed fact and speculation, but it wasn't the biblical account.
>
> My son learned that evening that you can't believe everything you hear or read—even if it's a "true" show. He knows he has to check things in the Bible for himself. A startling lesson to learn at seven, but I'd rather have my son disillusioned with TV than with God.

Relationship Rule Number Two: Having fun creates the right atmosphere for teachable moments.

If your children know you can relax and just play, they will see you in a whole new light—especially if you do something funny like putting colored cellophane wrappers on the light bulbs. Even teens appreciate a zany sense of humor and a change of atmosphere, though they might not show it at first.

Be sure there are times in your family life when you watch a movie, just for fun. When you have a water fight, just for fun. When you pitch a tent and sleep in the backyard, just for fun.

Here are more ideas:

- Do you eat fast food? Next time you go, take a child with you, but blindfold him first. See if he can figure out where you are by asking the cashier questions.
- At the dinner table have a contest to see who can create the longest sentence with words that start with the letter "B."
- Put green food coloring in the orange juice.
- Go to the library and check out the music from old Disney movies. Sing the songs in the car.
- Learn to talk with a phony accent or make up a secret family language.
- Have a whipped cream fight or a sock war.
- Go on a scavenger hunt.
- Visit a pet store and hold a snake.
- Play hide-and-seek outside.

Once you begin to have fun together, your kids will be relaxed and open—ready for a teachable moment. (See chapter 6 for suggestions on how to plan some fun times.)

Jim Weidmann does everything with just a little fanfare. At his house everyone plays Pente, a strategy game that uses pretty glass ovals as markers. Instead of just playing for fun, he's turned the Pente matches into an event by putting in just a little effort. He took an old wrestling trophy and glued two shiny Pente orbs onto it. The Pente winner for the evening gets to keep the trophy until the next match. As the trophy passes from bedroom to bedroom, so does the anticipation and excitement of the next Pente event.

Relationship Rule Number Three: Developing biblically based house rules creates a context for teachable moments. Unnecessary, legalistic, or seemingly capricious discipline or control creates a roadblock on the path to a smooth relationship.

Ask yourself what the basis is for each of your house rules and do away with those that can be let go without compromising biblical standards. For example, do your kids really need to put their shoes in their room, or couldn't you just put a box by the front door

The Silent Treatment

My girls are now 16 and 12. Usually, they are excited when I get home; the house is full of chatter. But when I'm not spending enough time with them, their trust in me diminishes along with their enthusiasm. Normally, I have a dozen or so questions to ask about their day—questions relevant to their world, not mine.

Right now Janae is all caught up in the excitement of homecoming. I'm proud to admit that I know the buzz about who is going and even which restaurants they're going to. I know which guys and girls, by name, are going to the dance together. If I weren't spending enough time with Janae, I wouldn't even know what to ask, let alone be privy to that information. When I'm not in tune with my daughters, I'm given the silent treatment. And if you think that teens sometimes say alarming things, try having them say nothing at all. To me, that's even more frightening, because you don't know what's going on.

where they can slip them off when they come in the door? Do the trashcans really have to be out by 6 A.M. on Saturday, or can your teen sleep in and put them out at 8:15? Why can't your daughter wear her favorite blue jeans to school five days in a row if she washes them every evening?

Of course, your child has to learn to take care of her things and become a responsible person, but reevaluate your house rules and see if you can simplify them into categories that reflect values found in the Bible. Instead of 50 rules, have four or five based on positive character traits. Here are some suggestions:

1. Put others first. Be respectful.
2. If you use it, put it away. Be responsible.
3. Work before play. Be diligent.
4. Be true to your word. Be trustworthy.

If you've been lax about having meaningful conversations with your kids, try using these starter questions:

- Whom did you sit with at lunch today?
- What are your discussions about?
- What was the topic of the day?
- Did anything funny happen?
- Did anyone cry today? What about?

Once the conversation has started, here are some good follow-up questions:

- When that happened, how did you feel?
- Why do you think that?
- What basis are you using to take your position?
- If you had to do it all over again, what would you do differently?
- What would Jesus have done in that situation? Why?
- How do you think the other person felt?

—J.W.

Simplifying rules also helps cut down on nagging (which doesn't work anyway) and focuses on the real issues, such as honesty or respect. Isn't it more profitable to address the values of stewardship rather than the dirty socks under the table? If your rules are based on biblical values, when you enforce them, you'll be talking about issues of substance, cause and effect, real life, character.

Having biblically based rules will present many opportunities for teachable moments. If your children buy into and see the reasons behind your house rules, they are more likely to respect them and internalize them. If you can defuse the tension when you discipline, your children won't be so uptight when you give advice, and they will be more likely to listen when you present a teachable moment.

In your house you need to have a standard for right and wrong. My (Jim's) overall house rule comes from Joshua 24:15—"But as for me and my household, we will serve the LORD."

One day when Jacob was about 15, he was in his room listening to some music. He went downstairs and left his door open. I stuck my head inside to hear what he was playing, and I thought, *This is not honoring to God!*

I called him upstairs. "Hey, Jake," I said. "Just listen to those words."

"Aw, Dad," he said, "I love the beat; I don't listen to the words." *Yeah, sure, I believe that....* I explained, "The Bible says we should focus on what's pure and right. These lyrics are *not* pure and right, and so I'm asking you to get rid of the CD." It went in the trash, and he's never bought another CD that's not honoring to God.

If you want some practice turning house rules into a forum for a teachable moment, consider this scenario:

Seven-year-old Jarrod has been home from school for over an hour. You've talked about his day, and he's eaten an apple and a handful of caramel corn. You've just finished doing the dishes when you notice his backpack on the dining room table and his shoes next to the TV.

You respond:

a. *"What is your backpack doing on the table?"*

b. *"Why did you just leave your shoes in the living room? Do you think I'm your personal maid?"*

c. *"If you don't pick up those items by the time I count to five, you're not getting any dessert tonight."*

d. *"Jarrod, you need to show me that you're responsible with your things before I'll let you have responsibility with the computer."*

The first two options invite a sarcastic response. Can't you just hear a kid answering the question "What's that backpack doing on the table?" with this answer: "The backpack stroke!" Answer *c* is much better, but still not on the mark; it links a behavior with a reward, but how many years can you count to five in your strictest schoolmarm voice and still be taken seriously? That answer may get results, but it doesn't leave any room for a discussion. Answer *d* is the best because it links behavior with a character trait. Mom is still being firm and setting boundaries, but it's clear that she wants Jarrod to focus on a character trait, not merely a "rule" that says where his stuff is or isn't allowed to be. After Jarrod puts his backpack and shoes away, he'll ask for permission to play a computer game, and he may be ready to hear a teachable moment about how God rewards those who are faithful in little things (Luke 16:10-12).

If done lovingly, discipline times can become the foundation for a future teachable moment, which can enhance a relationship, not detract from it.

Relationship Rule Number Four: Acceptance of your children helps them accept your teachable moments.

On a beautiful summer day at an outdoor carnival, a mother scolded her four-year-old daughter for being too frightened to get on a Ferris wheel. "Honestly," she said, "I wonder why I bother with you at all. You're ruining the whole day."

An outsider might point out that the day still had many possibilities: the basketball throw; the petting zoo; a nice slow train ride; or a big, fluffy wad of cotton candy. Why judge the entire carnival on the basis of one event? Just like a turn on the Ferris wheel, that will get you nowhere.

It's natural for parents to have expectations for their children, but it becomes damaging to a relationship when specific expectations or criteria become the only measure of success. From a relationship perspective, that will get you nowhere. If the child measures up, he'll resent the pressure. If he doesn't measure up, the pain of the parent's rejection may last a lifetime.

Thirty-four-year-old Mike E.'s father never could accept his son's acne, for example. After a recent visit home to see his parents, Mike

A.J.'s Alternatives

A.J. has a great smile and a voice that has just a hint of a rasp. He gels his hair so that it sticks straight up like a porcupine's quills, as is the current fashion. He's a handsome 12-year-old boy and drives the girls to distraction—but not with his good looks. In a normal classroom A.J.'s noisy fidgeting distracts them from their studies.

At five, he was kicked out of Sunday school and suspended from kindergarten. By sixth grade, he was so angry and frustrated with school that he wanted to quit; to him it seemed his whole life was consumed with homework, homework, and more homework. Recently he's begun attending an alternative school where he's just one of the ADHD crowd, and he is able for once to keep up with his studies. Alternatives work for A.J.

His mother has spent years making their home an alternative to the world from which A.J. is usually rejected. At home, he's safe and accepted the way he is. In fact, after the few times A.J. has run away from school, he has sprinted home like a colt bolting for the barn. In the neighborhood, he's recalled the way his father introduced him to a golf buddy: "This here is my son, Mike. I never could get him to wash his face. That's why he's got those pitted scars." Talk about scars—Mike's emotional pain runs deep; he never felt accepted by his father because he wasn't handsome physically. Though Mike has become a successful and caring high school principal, he still longs to be cared for by his father.

God made your child for a unique purpose; learn to appreciate what good qualities your child has instead of dwelling on the areas where he or she disappoints you or is not like you. Let your kids lead you into the areas they have an interest in and you will see their good qualities shine.

I (Jim) was born and raised in a locker room. But neither of my sons is athletic. They are not built mentally or physically for football.

quite popular, and kids can always be seen coming and going from his house. There is a warm and welcome atmosphere with lots of kid-friendly food and exciting things to do, such as jump on the trampoline, ride bikes, or play with electronic games. At home, his high energy and talkative nature make him a fun playmate. When a new kid moves in, A.J. is sure to know about it and invite that child to play.

A.J. brings them all to Wyldlife (the middle school version of Young Life). Most of the kids have never heard the gospel, and it's the first exposure they've had to Jesus' salvation message. A.J. is able to bring so many people because he's learned at home how to accept people as they are. He recently encouraged a seventh-grade-girl to turn to God for help with her problems.

Because of his parents' example, A.J. knows that everybody needs an alternative to the world's values—a place of unconditional acceptance. Everybody needs a home.

—mkh

When I realized that, I thought, *What am I going to do now? If I try to get my boys into my world, football, they will be killed.* Football would have set them up for failure, and I knew my relationship with them would suffer as a result.

So instead of hoping my boys would one day be scouted for a pro football team, I let them be scouts—Boy Scouts. Once a month I entered the wilderness with 40 boys armed with knives. I got it all: wind, rain, snow, blisters, and bears. I had a great time with my boys.

If they had pursued football, they would have felt they could not meet my expectations, and as a result, they would never feel they had my approval. They would not feel like they received my blessing. The Boy Scouts helped them to learn self-control and discipline. It also helped us discover each other. What I didn't count on from the experience was that my Jacob and Joshua would develop this internal pride that their dad was scoutmaster. They received my approval and blessing—and I received theirs.

If your child feels loved just the way he is, then he'll be more willing to believe that God loves him, which is the first step toward a healthy spiritual relationship. If he feels accepted by you, he will probably accept a teachable moment when it is offered.

Relationship Rule Number Five: Asking for your child's opinion will encourage him or her to accept yours.

"I am up to my armpits in work, Jasmine," her mother said, holding out a to-do list. "I don't see how I can scoot you over to Supercuts this afternoon. Do you see a way out of this mess?"

Jasmine, age 13, scans the to-do list. "I can vacuum—except for Bailey's room; I'm not picking up all his Lego stuff—and I'll put away the laundry. If you drop me off at Supercuts, you can stop by Sam's Club and then come back for me. Would that create enough time?"

Jasmine's mother is wise. She needed help with the chores, but instead of telling Jasmine what to do, she found a way for her daughter to volunteer as well as take part in the day's scheduling. All that with one simple question: "Do you see a way?…"

You can be a firm parent and still use opinions and suggestions from your kids and teens as long as they know you have the final say. For example, Jasmine's mother has not lost the right to insist Jasmine vacuum the entire house—including Bailey's room—or she can reject Jasmine's plan entirely. But by listening to your child's rationale, you can find out a lot about what's in her heart and mind. If you respect their opinions and even solicit their advice, children, especially teens, feel as if they are contributing to the decision-making process and will invest themselves more willingly into the final outcome.

Jasmine's mother also uses questions when she presents a teachable moment. "I just read that a California circuit court ruled that the phrase 'under God' is unconstitutional in the Pledge of Allegiance. Would it make any difference to you if the phrase is cut?"

In this way, she is letting Jasmine express her perspective. Later, Mom can shape the teachable moment to appeal to or correct Jasmine's point of view. If Jasmine answers, "It would make me sad, but it really doesn't affect me all that much, Mom. I know that God is in control no matter what is in the pledge," her mother's answer will address a different point than if Jasmine says, "You know, that phrase is meaningless anyway. Hardly anybody believes in God anymore."

By asking for your child's opinions and viewpoints, no matter what they are, you are strengthening the relationship as well as preparing for future teachable moments.

Relationship Rule Number Six: Anger sabotages relationships and derails a teachable moment.

Most kids wish their parents would lose their tempers—and never find them again. But tempers always seem to flare up in unexpected places—Sunday morning before church, on family vacations, and at the dinner table. James 1:19 should be the motto for every parent:

"Everyone should be quick to listen, slow to speak and slow to become angry."

Jim Weidmann offers the following anger no-no's for parents who want a good relationship with their child:

Never attack your child verbally or physically. Instead of condemnation, he or she needs guidance to move from a bad choice to a better one. And never discipline your children, especially teens, in front of their peers. Their humiliation will likely lead them to return the "favor" with belligerence. If an issue needs to be dealt with immediately, take him or her to another room and speak quietly there.

Having a good relationship with your older children or teens doesn't mean you stop being a parent. If you've established a boundary and your child deliberately crosses it, the boundary must be

Coaching Strategies

After being a coach at the middle and high school levels for 25 years, I've picked up a few lessons that have helped me be a better parent.

Coaching has taught me how to be more objective about my children's successes and failures. I see many parents on the sidelines who can't separate their own self-esteem from their child's performance. They are living through their children, and the pressure is so intense that their children aren't allowed to fail. I call them the "chess parents." No matter what sport or position their child plays, he or she is really only a pawn in the parent's game of life.

A good coach can see that failure often leads to growth and creates a spirit in the child that makes him or her more teachable and a better team player. We sometimes want our kids to be perfect, to drive them to success. By doing that, however, we lose the opportunity to teach them through their mistakes.

A good parent-coach makes sure home is a safe place to fail. When kids go to the sidelines, they need to find encouragement and motivation, to enforced. Author Josh McDowell reminds us that rules without relationship lead to rebellion, but so also does relationship without rules.

Avoid responding to your adolescent's behavior in an adolescent way. Don't trade insults. Don't chase a sullen, stomping son and deliver a tirade to his retreating back. It's not worth ruining a relationship just so you can have the last word or glaring look. Disengage from the battle, if necessary, and tell your child that you'll discuss the subject later.

If you as parents frustrate your child, you will not have earned the right in the relationship to share your faith or values. If the relationship is modeled after the one set by the heavenly Father, however, you stand a good chance of eliminating frustration. A good parent-child relationship is based on:

talk with someone who believes they can do it. If they are wounded, they need to be patched up and sent back out to try again. If you give your child criticism at that point, you will crush his or her spirit.

But that doesn't mean you can't be tough.

I grew up with five brothers, zero sisters. I can't remember a time when I didn't have to fight or compete. My first two children are daughters, and they have a softer emotional makeup than my brothers. (Also a softer left hook!) My tendency was to coddle them until I realized that wouldn't work in the long run. Coaching has taught me how to be tough if it's for a higher cause. Coaching has allowed me to balance my tenderness with discipline.

When you have children's highest interests in mind, you can teach them to be tough. You listen to their emotions and acknowledge them, but you don't necessarily give in to them. That's part of teaching them self-control. The practice field has to prepare them for the real game, and being a Christian in the real world is tough.

—Jeff Leeland

- unconditional love: "I will love you no matter what."
- being available for your child: "I will be there for you in whatever way you need."
- having your child's best interests in mind: "I will not think primarily about your comfort or happiness, but first about your character."
- grace: "I will forgive you as Christ forgives me."

It is normal for your child to be frustrated with you, but he or she should never be forced to the point of exasperation. Frustration is appropriate when you enforce boundaries or discipline—after all, these are children, and they are learning consequences to their choices. Frustration is also expected when your child can't see the long-term benefits of obedience or discipline, or when your child experiences disappointment. But exasperation has a different flavor; it tastes bitter and resentful. You trigger it when you handle your child's frustration inappropriately. Then no one wins. You need to begin immediately to restore the respect factor and your child's confidence so you can continue in your spiritual training.

Your sons and daughters need you to be a parent. On the other hand, being a parent doesn't mean you have to be unlikable or harsh. Based on his years in youth work as well as parenting, author and speaker Joe White says in *Parents' Guide to the Spiritual Mentoring of Teens*, "When you like someone, you obey him because you want to. Likable parents don't scold; they speak with grace. They don't lecture; they serve. Likable parents don't act bitter; they discipline and forgive. They don't give kids a list when they come home from school; they give them hugs."

If you keep your temper tempered, your children will be able to trust you to act consistently and fairly. They will respect your advice and teachable moments better if they are confident you are on their side.

Every Parent Is a Coach

Three more easily identifiable parenting styles can be added to the list that was started in chapter 2 (The Wallet, The Pew, and the others). They are…

- The Rock—the parent who is always there to lay down the law, but that's about it. The whole house atmosphere revolves around rules and discipline. Sure, The Rock is stable and trustworthy, but who would share anything with a parent as hard as granite?
- The Cheerleader—the parent who thinks everything his or her child does is fantastic. There's a lot of fun and enthusiasm—but no boundaries. This parent does back flips to make sure the children like him or her. He or she does not get much respect and often wonders why.
- The Coach—this parent is available in the game of life. Through respect, he or she can expect directions to be followed. A coach makes sure there are plenty of chances for the players to get it right. This parent gives heartfelt attention to morale and can be counted on to throw a team party when the children succeed. He or she is also the last to leave the locker room of despair when things go wrong.

The three examples above are, of course, stereotypes. Most people will exhibit a variety of parenting styles throughout their "career" as a parent. The goal is to be aware of your styles and try to mold them to the biblical standard. We can't take a break from parenting until we are perfect, but we can adjust when we see an area in which we need to mature. One "cheerleader" mother of three tells how she's trying to incorporate discipline into her parenting style:

> I grew up in a house where my father was most like The Rock when it came to discipline. You can take your dad out of the

Army, but it's hard to take the Army out of your dad. During my elementary years I was burdened by all the rules in the house and intimidated by his military-style discipline; therefore, I spent a good part of my life trying not to "wake the sleeping dragon" and incur his finger-wagging lectures. In a deliberate attempt to be less rules-oriented, I oftentimes don the uniform of a cheerleader with pom-poms waving and lots of cheering. I want to offer my kids fun, encouragement, and an upbeat atmosphere, so I'm more flexible about house rules than my father was. But when it comes to a relationship or respect issue and my children prod me, I'm likely to come at them breathing fire as my father did, because I will not tolerate disobedience in those areas.

At times I must seem like the character Princess Fiona in the movie *Shrek,* who can't decide if she wants to be the epitome of sweetness or an ogre. But I am working on being more predictable and deliberate in my discipline approaches. I know to apologize when I've been too harsh in the way I disciplined (I don't apologize for the fact that I disciplined), and that helps keep the relationship steady, plus it's a good example. If my teenage daughter snaps at me or my husband, she's also learned to make a quick apology and start the conversation over, not only out of a fear of consequences, but also out of a true desire to be godly.

If the description of The Rock matches your parenting style, don't worry; it isn't chiseled in stone. With God's help, you can intentionally learn to become more like The Coach and let the rules help the relationship instead of hinder it.

Or if you are too flexible and do a backbend every time your child pushes you, then admit it—you're a bit too much like The Cheerleader. Work on building some backbone. Children and teens *need* you to lovingly enforce boundaries; they *want* a just authority. If you exhibit weakness in the area of discipline, they will see your God as weak and want nothing to do with Him. If you act with the God-given authority you already have as a parent, your child will respect both you and God.

Obviously, The Coach is the model that most closely represents a biblical one, especially for older children. This parent is available, enforces standards of conduct, is committed to the long haul (eternity), encourages by coming alongside, and offers empathy. The Coach lets his or her children be starters and lets them call the shots when they are ready. Modeling your parenting style after a good coach will improve your relationship with your children and enhance the quality of your teachable moments.

When I (Jim) was at the Air Force Academy, I played for two different coaches. One was disciplined, and as a result, I became a disciplined player. My technique was great, but I didn't have much fun.

The other coach was different. He coached me through the heart, not through rules. That guy was a phenomenal motivator. During one game against Notre Dame, I was out there getting killed—this guy who was 50 percent bigger than I kept knocking me down as if I were his grandmother. I spent so much time on the ground that I had grass stains on my *back*.

I went over to the sidelines to tell the coach I was getting killed, and he said, "I've been watching you, Weidmann. While that guy is beating you up, he's not getting to the quarterback. And we're running right past them. Keep going."

As I went back on the field to lay down my life again, I was smiling, because I was playing from my heart. Rules will never give the same results.

By learning to be a good coach-parent, you can get maximum impact out of your discussions about God. When you use a teachable moment, your goal isn't to teach a list of rules, do's and don'ts. Your goal is to mold your children's hearts so that each one can become a starter on God's team.

Relationship Rebound

Relationship can cure the common coldness and resentfulness of teens. When I (Marianne) first met 13-year-old Claire B., a student in my journalism class at a home-school co-op, I saw a bright, happy-go-

Imagination Station

Knowing the difference between fantasy and reality is a key mental milestone in every child's life. It's not uncommon for parents to be worried about a child who lies and tells tall tales even through the second grade. Right now, Justin and Kendrick both lie to avoid punishment. They blame each other for spilled drinks and torn books, even if the other twin could not possibly have been the culprit. The other day, I noticed Kendrick's pants were wet. I said in surprise, "Did you pee in your pants?" He looked at me, brow furrowed, with seriousness. "I didn't do it," he whispered. "It was Justin."

To keep your relationship smooth until your children know the difference between pretending and lying, go easy on the fantasy fibs. There's a marked difference between kids who lie to avoid punishment—"I didn't knock over the lamp. It must have been the hamster."—and those who tell a fantasy fib, such as "We went to the zoo, and my mommy let me play in the gorilla cage. We had a birthday party, and Fred, the king gorilla, gave me a motorcycle."

I'd overheard five-year-old Danielle "lie" to cashiers at the grocery store or strangers at the library. "I have 11 brothers and sisters, and we live on 20 acres in the woods," she'd brag. "We play cowboys and Indians every day. I have a horse, three ducks, and a goat." In reality she was an only child, lived lucky girl. But I soon learned that Claire wasn't happy-go-lucky about her home life. In fact, her biggest fantasy was to run away. Frustration was written all over her expressive face whenever she discussed her parents. She explains, "I was exasperated with all the rules and felt like no one was listening to me. It seemed like my parents stayed up at night discussing ways to provoke me."

Claire's unhappiness was no surprise to her mother either. Robin confided that Claire had been resentful of parental authority for about

in the suburbs, and had only one small dog. But I always thought the tall tales were harmless—until I got the call from her kindergarten teacher.

"Mrs. Hering?"

"Yes..."

"It's Mrs. Hayden. Danielle says she has a heart condition, and she can't play with the other children outside or she'll get very sick."

"She said that?"

"Yes. You never mentioned it, but because it was such a serious thing, I thought I'd call and check. It's not true is it? I mean she looks fine...."

Danielle might not have a heart condition, but her teacher was sure to have one if I didn't clear up this story.

"Danielle is fine. She has a trifle overactive imagination, but other than that, she's in good health."

The previous weekend my kindergartner had been mildly obsessed with an "Adventures in Odyssey" episode in which Whit was stuck inside the Imagination Station with a "heart condition." I could have scolded her for telling such a worrying lie, but I didn't, mostly because I was laughing too hard, and also because I knew from her character that it wasn't going to be repeated. My instincts to be lenient were correct. We've never had another episode like that.

—mkh

a year. Around her parents she was sullen, sometimes sneaky, proving herself disrespectful at many a turn. Robin's goal was to protect Claire until she learned better values; unless she did so, Robin feared that Claire would make some big mistakes.

Out of concern and a desire to provide a wholesome environment, her mother and father selected her clothes, her social groups, her

Voice Over

Those of us who have lived with an angry parent also know the angry voices—yes, the voices from your past that still talk to you, especially when you're frustrated or discouraged. The voices that say…

- I can't believe you did that!
- How can you be so stupid?
- It's all your fault.
- Why can't you do anything right?
- Well, you've blown it again.
- I can't wait until you kids move out of the house.
- You'll never get a date if you act like that.
- You'll never be able to keep your room clean.
- You're never going to amount to anything.
- I wish you'd never been born.

The dialog varies, but they all translate into "You're worthless." It used to be that way when I was tired or frustrated with my kids, I heard one of these voices spewing out of my mouth. I would have to stop and immediately apologize.

Now I have made saying good things a habit; I've dubbed over the old recordings. Here are some voice-over lines to replace the ones you may have heard as a kid:

- I like the way you did that.
- You're a good friend. I can see why so-and-so likes you.

coursework, her movies, her music. Because they wanted Claire to follow the courtship model for finding a husband, they limited her phone conversations with boys to five minutes. Robin also tried to cut off ties with Claire's favorite friend because Robin felt she was "a bad influence"; when the two were together at the friend's house, Robin feared the teens talked about boys and watched inappropriate movies.

- You worked hard on that, I can tell.
- Your eyes sparkle when you laugh.
- You make me happy, or proud, or…
- That was a good decision.
- What a helpful person you've become.
- God is proud of the way you handled that.
- I can see love (or joy, or peace, or patience, or kindness, or gentleness, or self-control) in you. That's a godly way to be.
- I appreciate that you were quiet.
- You must be disappointed with that outcome. But I'm sure you'll do a better job next time. What kind of help do you need?
- You got along well with your brother/sister today. Thanks.
- You put a lot of thought into that, didn't you?
- I'm so glad you're in our family.
- God knew exactly what He was doing when he made you; you're just right.
- I love you.

The best part about compliments is that anger isn't the only thing that repeats itself. Compliments also prove that what goes around comes around. When you're kind, your kids start talking like that too. When one of them says something nice to me like "That was a fun trip to the movies, Dad," it's like stuffing a sock in the mouth of the old voice; the anger is momentarily silenced.

—anonymous

In order to keep Claire out of trouble, Robin gave her the first fruits of her time, money, and spiritual energy. You couldn't ask for a more dedicated mother. She home schooled Claire, sewed clothes for Claire, drove all over town for Claire. Robin was an experienced mother who wasn't afraid to use consistent discipline, and she read and reread all the Christian parenting books she could find to absorb the principles on how to pass on a spiritual legacy. She prayed and asked for support from her friends and pastors. They moved away from the suburbs to a remote place in the country and bought Claire goats, a dog, and a horse. This mother was doing her best to raise a godly child—in fact, she had most of her parenting act on par with Scripture. She was only missing a good relationship, a way to begin letting Claire have some control, fun, and share her opinions.

After watching *Stepmom*, a movie that portrays a woman who becomes a valued member of the family by bringing much-needed joy, Robin decided she needed to be "more like that." More like that meant having more fun, such as playing sixties music and singing and dancing in the living room. More like that meant taking a trip to Prince Edward Island. More like that meant listening to Claire's opinions about her friends and music. More like that meant letting Claire highlight her hair.

Robin also began to listen to Claire's favorite songs on the secular radio and learned the lyrics. They discussed the bad ones and chose to avoid them, but they both enjoyed it when a good melody came on and would sing together in the car.

Robin gave up sewing Claire's clothes and let her daughter choose her own outfits. They established modesty guidelines and let Claire's conscience be the measure instead of Mom's. Sure, a couple of skirts might have been a tad short, but overall, Claire made godly choices and relished the freedom to be responsible for her actions. Suddenly, Claire felt like she was a person, not just a child-rearing project.

Claire's response to the change in her relationship with her mother was "Wow, maybe she *can* understand me. I don't have to fight so hard to be heard." And Claire began to listen more carefully to her parents. By the time Claire entered high school, she had learned how to communicate with her parents without being rude and to present logical arguments when discussing issues. Claire also showed respect for the Bible's authority, and her conscience was strong enough to keep her out of trouble. As a result, she earned the privilege of going to public school.

Public high school offered the evil her parents imagined it would with the availability of drugs, the sexually charged atmosphere, the crassness, the meanness. At this point, Claire realized just how difficult living a Christian life could be, and she began seeking advice from her parents, especially Robin. Even though Claire still sometimes acted out, she had absorbed her parents' values, and when given the chance, she stuck with them. She chose not to follow the wild crowd (well, she did get a belly button ring after talking it over with her parents) and had a successful high school career that resulted in a college scholarship.

I saw Claire and Robin just a few weeks ago. Soon Claire's fantasy will come true—when she moves into the dorm and out of the house! But she has one regret—she'll miss her mom, her "best friend."

CHAPTER SIX

The Catalyst: The Second Component of a Teachable Moment

Jeff Leeland had a medical crisis in his family that became the catalyst for many teachable moments. His newborn son, Michael, developed leukemia a few months after birth. The doctors believed it to be treatable, and Michael's sister Amy matched for a bone marrow transplant. That was the good news. The bad news was that Jeff had switched jobs just after Michael's birth and his new health insurance had a 12-month waiting period for transplants. It was doubtful Baby Michael could wait 12 days, let alone the several months it would be until he qualified for the operation. He was dying, and there was no way the Leelands could pay the $175,000 cash deposit required for the operation.

Or was there a way? Through the courage and determination of the students at Kamiakan Junior High School in Kirkland, Washington, the money was raised. It came in dollar by dollar as kids emptied their piggy banks or gave up their school dance money. Other students recruited help from the media and local businesses; even the employees at the insurance company donated money from their private funds when the corporate funds were contractually unavailable.

Through that crisis, the Leeland family learned that God does indeed provide and cares for every detail of their lives. Jeff, his wife, and his five children will never doubt the words of Jesus in Matthew 10:29, 31, "Are not two sparrows sold for a penny? Yet not one of them will fall to the ground apart from the will of your Father. So don't be afraid; you are worth more than many sparrows."

Most of the time when the phrase "teachable moment" is used, people think of their crisis moments and what they learned from them. And crises do create colorful memory flags that wave at the top of the mast. The story about John and Austin Benge is another dramatic example. How many times do you expect your house to be burned down? You'd certainly have a tendency to remember that life event. And who will forget September 11? The violent surprise attack on the World Trade Center towers and the Pentagon will remain an example of pure evil for generations to come.

I (Jim) have also used a personal crisis to present a teachable moment. A few years ago I found myself unemployed. I knew God had led me to quit my job at IBM, but I didn't know yet where He wanted me. As the sole breadwinner for the family, I admit I was a little unnerved at the idea of being without a paycheck.

I didn't want the children to worry, though, so I put together a family night and talked to my kids about needing to trust God even when they don't know what is going to happen. Christians have to walk in faith, trusting God to provide. The verses we studied were part of Jesus' Sermon on the Mount: "So do not worry, saying, 'What shall we eat?' or 'What shall we drink?' or 'What shall we wear?' For the pagans run after all these things, and your heavenly Father knows that you need them. But seek first his kingdom and righteousness, and all these things will be given to you as well" (Matthew 6:31-33). Then I used my job situation as an example. I knew that God would provide for our needs, and I wanted my children to watch and see what God would do; I didn't want them to "miss the show"!

God used this crisis as a teachable moment for me as well. I asked my children, "Aren't you concerned that your dad doesn't have a job?" They came back and said, "No—you're our dad. You'll take care of us." Then God checked me in my heart: "Jim, do you trust me like your children trust you? Do you trust that I have a plan for you?"

Some weeks later I was offered a job opportunity at Focus on the Family. God knew I was ready to be in full-time ministry, and He had worked out many details to get me to this point in my life. My kids watched it all unfold from the best spot in the house. They had a front-row seat to see how God would keep His promise and provide a job.

But I don't wait for a crisis to find a reason to talk about God with my family. If I did that, we might not be ready when the crises come. A trial may break my family instead of build it up unless we have a firm foundation, unless I've impressed the commandments on their hearts. I've seen too many people suffer disappointments with God and leave the faith because they don't understand His true purpose. I'm not willing to take that chance with my family. I remind my children about God's faithfulness and commandments every opportunity I get. I use teachable moments even in non-crisis situations.

One way I do that is to look for everyday household catalysts and attach a biblical truth to them. Here are some suggestions:

- Occasionally, when I drop the kids off at school, I remind them that it's their job to "Go into all the world and preach the good news to all creation" (Mark 16:15).
- When they were younger and I'd help them with their bath, we'd sometimes talk about the concept of Jesus' blood cleansing us from our sins.

- The mirror in our bathroom represents the passage in James 1:23-24, "Anyone who listens to the word but does not do what it says is like a man who looks at his face in a mirror and, after looking at himself, immediately forgets what he looks like." I challenge my kids to use the Bible as a mirror. That's the image they are supposed to look at, and I hope that they will see themselves. If, after comparing themselves to Scripture and they find something out of place, they know to fix it, much as they would fix their hair before going to work or to school.
- One fun object lesson my kids really enjoyed was when I gave them each a baby bottle filled with chocolate milk and said, "Drink up." It's a lot more difficult to drink from a bottle than they thought it would be. After that we discussed the fact that

The Itsy-Bitsy Lesson

"The daddy longlegs is the most poisonous spider in the world," Danielle announced one day on the way to soccer practice.

I looked at her in the rearview mirror. What? I don't think that's true; it sounds like an urban legend to me. Those spiders are crawling all over the basement and backyard. And I'm sure my little brother ate one once.

"They really are. Nicole told me," she continued.

Ah-hah. Nicole the wonder babysitter has spoken.

"They're the most poisonous, but not the most dangerous because their teeth aren't sharp enough to penetrate human skin."

"Hey," I piped in, "that's like being a Christian. Satan is dangerous, and he can bother us, but he can't kill us because Jesus protects us."

"I never looked at it that way," Danielle said.

Neither had I. Thanks, God. It turns out that the part about the spider is not true, but still Your love is.

—mkh

baby Christians crave milk, but as they mature, Christians are supposed to crave solid food. You can discuss this at any mealtime.

- Out of the blue, I'll ask my kids, "What are you billboarding today?" because we are supposed to reflect Christ, be the image of Christ in everything we do, including our style of dress. At Jacob and Janae's high school, the other kids wear "uniforms." You can spot the basketball players with their baggy shorts, the skateboarders with the saggy pants, and the kids who are into dark music by their unkempt hair and the demonic graphic designs on their T-shirts; these "uniforms" reflect the subcultures that the owners value.

You can also turn negative catalysts into positive teaching times. Youth speaker Josh McDowell tells how one day he sat with his kids in a public place that had been vandalized by offensive graffiti. Instead of trying to shield them from the profanity and quickly ushering them to more neutral territory, he pointed it out to them. He answered their questions about the "colorful" language and helped them identify the artist's distorted values.

Josh hadn't planned to deliver an object lesson that day. But when the opportunity presented itself, he took full advantage of it.

Even life's little disasters can provide chances to create a strong teachable moment. Hannah recalls what happened when she was 15.

I tried to sneak the family car out of the garage late at night. I planned to have it back before anyone noticed, and I guess I was thinking too far ahead or something. I went to back out, but it didn't go backward. It went forward instead, right through the wall of my sister's bedroom. Luckily, she was away at college. But I just shut off the car and started crying. My dad came out and saw me, but if he was angry, he didn't show it. He made sure I was all right and helped me get the car back in the garage. Then, over the next few months, he rebuilt the wall and we actually repainted the room together.

Hannah's dad made that time count. His response left her with a lasting image of her father's love and patience that she'll never forget.

Ready or Not, Catalysts Come

Sometimes things happen in the world around us that must be addressed through a teachable moment, even if you feel your child isn't ready or even if you're not ready.

Kurt Bruner, vice president of resource development at Focus on the Family, was eating his breakfast when his son Kyle, then 11, gave him some more to chew on. "Can I have the paper for the horoscope section?"

Holding back a choking cough, Kurt said, "Why do you want that?"

"I have an assignment for school where we have to write a horoscope."

Kurt became agitated, and at first Kyle thought he had done something wrong. After reassuring Kyle that he wasn't in trouble, Kurt began a discussion about what horoscopes and divination are, even though Kurt would have liked to wait until Kyle was older. He told Kyle that those things try to take the place of God's wisdom, to answer questions that only God can and should answer. Then Kurt had a subsequent "teachable moment" with Kyle's teacher.

This type of catalyst is a mini-crisis. While you have no choice but to explain the death of a sibling or address the fact that your house has burned down, you can choose to ignore the milder crises that come your way. Kurt could have told his son to "never mind" the horoscope project and dealt only with the teacher. But unless your child is very young, it is foolish to gloss over something because it creates a "forbidden" or "grownup" aura. Skirting the issue sends a message that this subject is not to be discussed at home. As a result, when your child needs information about it, he or she may not turn to you but rather to another source of information, such as peers or the Internet. You need to ask yourself where you want your child learning about drugs, sex, homosexuality, or Ouija boards.

That doesn't mean if your seven-year-old child wants to know about demon possession that you rent *The Exorcist* and watch it together. You need only to satisfy his or her curiosity with age-appropriate material, starting with the biblical perspective.

Here's another story about a mini-crisis shared by a basketball-coach dad who would have rather avoided the situation.

> One winter during a tournament, one of the boys on our team received a fat lip, another a black eye, and my son was pushed from behind milliseconds before taking an open shot. All three players were back on the court minutes after their mishaps, but only in a few instances did the referee call a foul against the opposing team.
>
> Coaches, parents, and players alike should know that roughness is sometimes part of the competition. Unfortunately, a parent on an opposing team didn't like the physical nature of the game that afternoon. He approached me just after the game's close. He was yelling, threatening, and complaining that our boys had played too rough a game. I tried to politely point out that the referee had called many more fouls on their team, we'd had no players removed from the game, and that whenever you have 10 kids all vying for a basketball in a tiny space, there's bound to be some contact. But that was when I noticed the watery, reddish eyes with the glazed expression.
>
> *Great. I'm gonna be killed right in front of my child like that hockey coach last spring.*
>
> A friend (six-foot-six and at least 220) helped keep the man from escalating the discussion into a physical altercation, however, and I didn't die. Afterward, the man even apologized

for his outburst. But my friend and I both more than suspected the complainer was drunk.

Unfortunately, my son witnessed it all. Fortunately, we could talk about it. Later on we were able to discuss the negative effects of alcohol and why the Bible says it's evil to drink too much. We took the lesson one step farther when I encouraged him to find compassion for the man who came drunk to his son's basketball game.

Question Catalysts

Because the ultimate goal of a teachable moment is to have a conversation with your child about God or biblical truth, often the best catalysts are the very questions your kids ask you. That way, you know you have their attention and that their curiosity is aroused. As we saw in chapter 4, the trick to this type of catalyst is creating a good relationship with your children so they feel free to ask those questions.

Most small children begin early to pose those deep questions about God. One particular point that tends to confuse kids is the concept of "Jesus living in our hearts." Four-year-old Mitchell Donohue presented this question: "Mom, if my heart is the size of my fist and Jesus lives in my heart, He doesn't have much room, does He?" Three-year-old Luke Prince had similar concerns. He wanted to know, "If Jesus lives in my heart, does He bite?" Carolyn Eklund, a grandmother of six, told about her grandson's struggle with an invisible God: "Our grandson, then four years old, took a trip with his grandfather. After the plane had taken off, Jacob said, 'Grampy, how high does this thing have to go before we see Jesus?' "

Sometimes children's questions aren't so direct. To find out what they really want to know, you need to ask them some questions to clarify the issue. For example, I (Marianne) was driving 11-year-old Danielle on an errand when she asked, "Mom, why do boys and girls act that way?" I thought, *Which "that way"?* There are so many bizarre boy and girl "that ways" in middle school that I couldn't begin to answer without more information. I said, "Why do you ask that?"

"Well," she said, "there were these two eighth-graders, and they were yelling at each other in the hall. Before the teacher could close the door, I heard the boy say to the girl that she was a prostitute, and she yelled back and said, 'I am not a prostitute!'"

Oh. That way!

Then I knew which way the discussion needed to turn. Certainly, sex was involved in that conversation, and just as certainly, love wasn't. We talked about the double standard in our society that implies it is more acceptable for boys to have premarital sex than girls. I explained that if a girl has sex with a boy, he's likely to turn against her afterward, as was illustrated by the conversation she heard in the hallway and in the biblical account of Amnon and Tamar (2 Samuel 13). I also made it clear that the Bible holds men and women to the same standard of purity. There is no double standard in the Bible—only God's standard.

Other catalysts may be the questions you ask your children. One time when Jacob came home, I (Jim) asked the usual, "Did anything exciting happen at school today?"

"No. Nothing happened."

"Pretty standard day, huh?"

"Yeah."

It was still early evening when I said, "Hey, Jake, let's go out and throw the football around." With each toss of the ball, I tossed him a new question: "So this was standard day; are you just going to forget it?"

"Yeah, it was pretty boring—hey, wait a minute. Dad, you're gonna love this...."

Then he launched into a story about four Mormons who approached him and shared their theology.

"Well, what did you do?" I asked.

"It was really interesting; they said that Jesus was a brother of Satan."

"And what did you say to those Mormons?" By this time, I was holding the football; Jacob had my full attention.

He went on, "I asked those guys, 'How could that be? Satan was a fallen angel. He was a created being. Jesus is part of the Trinity—He is the Creator.' And you know what, Dad? They had no answer."

A pretty standard day—I think not! If I hadn't intentionally gotten Jacob relaxed and asked those questions to draw the day's events out of him, I would have missed that story and the discussion we had afterward. If I hadn't asked those questions, I would have "dropped the ball" as a parent.

Jumpstart the Conversation

If you wait for catalysts or questions to spark a teachable moment, many of those will be negative. It's amazingly easy to find individuals and situations that reveal ungodly characteristics. To bring in healthy catalysts that provide positive teachable moments and examples of godly behavior, make sure the house is flooded with character-building books, audio recordings, music, videos, magazines, and computer software.

Rhonda Rhea, a pastor's wife, writer, speaker, and mother of five, tells how a song by the group Avalon touched her daughter's heart:

> One day my 11-year-old daughter, Allie, had "the look" that said something was on her mind. I asked what was going on in her life. Her eyes got huge, tears welled up, and her deep dimples crinkled. "I'm being challenged to believe the right way, to do the right thing. And God is working on my heart, helping me learn how to love Him more—He is real."
>
> "What is God using to do that?" I asked.

She didn't hesitate and said, "Music."

All the times in the car when we pop in a Christian tape or tune to a Christian radio station, we're planting messages. And right then, I had the privilege of seeing those messages blossom in my daughter's life.

Books with noble or Christian themes also offer catalysts to create positive teachable moments. Kurt Bruner and his family recently listened to the "Chronicles of Narnia" fantasy stories by C.S. Lewis. "In the book *The Last Battle* there's a great extended metaphor for heaven," he said. "The word *heaven* is not even mentioned in the book, but all my kids knew instinctively that is what was being presented. We've used that story as a springboard to discuss what it's going to be like when we get there."

You can also take hold of those hours spent traveling by playing thought-provoking audio recordings. Julie Lindeman, a Christian therapist and mother of three, had this experience a few years ago:

> I was driving across country with my three teenagers to be with extended family for the holidays. My children had been somewhat disgruntled with God since their father and I divorced a few years earlier, and they had little interest in things of Christ. To pass the hours on this 16-hour drive across the plains, I purchased the *Left Behind* and *Tribulation Force* audio books, which I nonchalantly put into the CD player to listen to. All three of my teens acted as if they were very involved in their own thing like listening to music on a Walkman, reading, or sleeping. But after the first three hours of listening to the book, I was changing the CD for disc two, and one of my children asked a couple of questions about the story. By the time our trip was over, we were all engaged in conversation about the Rapture, salvation, and God's plan. For the first time in years, they were all interested

and opening up to learning. I praise God for planting the idea in my head. Not only did He bring a teachable moment, but our trip seemed to take half the usual time.

Kids remember these times, especially if they occur on an ongoing basis. One college student recalls, "Before I got my driver's license, Daddy used to drive me about 10 minutes to school every morning. During this time, we would listen to Chuck Colson's *Breakpoint* commentary on the radio and then discuss the day's topic. These times helped me begin to understand the importance of having a Christian worldview, and I saw my daddy's passion for God's truth and how that relates to our culture."

Lissa Johnson, a mother of three, shares these ideas for starting "car-versations":

1. If you're ferrying a group of your teen's friends, listen. Let the conversation flow around you as if you weren't paying attention. If something comes up that could harm someone, step in and direct the

Breaking the Sound Barrier

Getting a son to talk at all, to share more than one syllable, is an art. And when you feel as if you aren't connected with your kids, it bugs you. My husband has discovered a secret to getting more than caveman-like grunts out of our boys. After our family devotion times, he tells the other four children to go to bed. Then he gives the one child who isn't communicating this deal: "You can stay up as late as you want as long as you keep talking. When you stop talking, then you have to go to bed." Talk about a conversation catalyst for a teachable moment! Because the child sees staying up late as a great privilege, he'll tell you just about anything you want to know, and a little bit more besides.

—Rhonda Rhea

conversation toward a point you'd like to make. For example, the group might be giggling about pulling a practical joke on an unpopular classmate. You can ask how the kids would feel if someone did that to them. This might lead to a discussion on valuing the differences among people instead of ridiculing them, as well as the fact that God loves each of us equally.

2. If you're listening to the car radio, discuss what you hear. Let's say the news tells of a professional football player who's been arrested for drunk driving. You can start a conversation by asking something like "How do you feel when someone you respect makes a mistake?"

3. Talk about what you see as you drive. For instance, you're looking for a parking space and spot a frustrated mother outside the grocery store, screaming at her child. Ask your teen, "What would you do in a situation like that? How could it be handled better?"

Creating Your Own Catalyst

When my (Jim's) daughter Joy was 12, like most kids her age she just wanted to fit in with the crowd. My wife, Janet, pointed out that peer pressure was a particular struggle for Joy and asked for my help. Since I didn't have time to wait for the correct catalyst to pop up, I created my own.

I decided to have a family night. While Joy was out of the room, I informed everyone else of a little game we were going to play called "Which Line Is Longest?" I told the rest of the family to fib and say that they thought the middle line was the longest, whether it really was or not.

When Joy joined the gathering, we started the game. I drew three lines on a large piece of paper—the longest line was the third one. I asked, "Which line is longest?" When I pointed to the first line, no one raised a hand. When I pointed to the middle line, the whole family raised their hands, including Joy.

"What about the last line?" I asked. No one raised a hand, including Joy.

Just to make sure there had been no chance of a visual mistake, I drew three more lines and asked, "Which line is longest?" Once again, everyone voted for the middle line—including Joy.

When I said, "Well, you were all wrong. The last line is the longest," Joy jumped up and said, "I knew it!"

The pressure was then on me to explain why she was wrong to be "in line" with her family when she knew they had made a mistake. We followed up the moment by discussing why she would sometimes need to be different from her peers—when she needed to "step out of line" to please God.

Kurt Bruner relates a teachable moment he created for his son Kyle:

> One evening, I turned a trip to McDonald's into a faith lesson for my then-seven-year-old son, Kyle. We piled into the van, and I handed him a simple hand-drawn map.
>
> "Okay, Kyle. It's up to you to make sure we get to McDonald's." I started the car and proceeded down our street. At the corner, I stopped and looked over my shoulder at him. "Where do I go now?"
>
> Kyle looked at his map. "You turn left."
>
> "Naw," I told him. "I think I know what I'm doing; I don't think I need to turn left." I turned right instead.
>
> Kyle burst out in frustration, "It says you're supposed to turn left."
>
> At the next point of decision, I did the same thing. Soon Kyle was really mad.
>
> When we ended up at a dead end, I said, "I guess I didn't know where I was going, did I?"
>
> "That's right, Dad, because you were supposed to follow the directions," Kyle shouted.

"Well, now what are we going to do?" I asked.

"Go back to the beginning and we'll follow the directions."

So that's what we did. We went back to the beginning. This time I followed the directions. During this second attempt at reaching McDonald's, we discussed what had occurred on our first trip.

"That's what happens when we don't obey the Bible," I told him. "When we think we know what we're doing and we don't follow the directions, we lose our way. The Scriptures are our directions for life."

An extra five minutes added onto an already planned trip became a powerful teachable moment.

Creating your own catalyst takes a bit of practice to perfect; I (Marianne) tried a few one summer and found the formula to success: simplicity. My number-one mistake was not keeping enough control over the catalysts; my second was making them too complex. One Saturday, I had a great idea, but it was doomed from the get-go. While we were going to garage sales, I gave Danielle five dollars and asked her to buy something that "represented" her. I was going to use what she purchased to make a point later in the afternoon.

As soon as the money was in her hand, she asked, "If I buy something for $4.95, can I keep the nickel?" I said yes. "What if it costs $2.25, can I keep $2.75?" I said no. "What if it costs $3.50?" and so it went. For about two hours, we drove from sale to sale, and she could not find anything that "represented" her. "What does it mean to 'represent' me?" she kept asking. "Does it have to be something to do with sports? What if I like something but it doesn't *exactly* represent me?" I was the only one who learned something that afternoon: Don't give an abstract task to a concrete thinker.

One of my successful planned teachable moments was a simpler endeavor, and there were no outside distractions or issues. I had my principle in hand based on Ecclesiastes 5:10, "Whoever loves money never has enough," or only God satisfies; worldly cravings just increase. The catalyst had a clear focus and was completely under my control. I used the twins.

While the boys sat on the couch watching TV, I gave Justin a small piece of candy. Jealous, Kendrick asked for a piece. I gave him a lollipop. When Justin saw the lollipop, he wanted one. I said, "But you already have a candy." He threw it away so he could get a bigger piece. But instead of a lollipop, I gave him a roll of Smarties. With lollipop in mouth, Kendrick saw the Smarties and asked for a roll too. When I gave Kendrick the roll, Justin yelled out, "Me too." I knew I'd made my point. They both had more candy than they'd seen since Easter, and yet they clamored for more.

After letting them choose two pieces each and putting the rest of the candy away, I tossed Danielle some candy and asked, "Do you think they'll be happy as long as they know I have more candy to give?"

"No," she said.

"Let's say that they keep acting this way all their lives and never know God. What if they grow up and want money?" I asked. "Will they keep demanding more, even if they have enough?"

"Yes," she said.

"What's the only thing that will stop someone from wanting more and more worldly things?"

"God."

A simple catalyst paired with a simple truth makes a simply beautiful teachable moment.

Family Nights

As with Jim Weidmann's example of the family night on peer pressure, planned teachable moments work best when you have a group of people to participate. When people think of devotions, somehow they get stuck on the idea of a reading a long Scripture passage, asking some questions, and then closing in a solemn prayer. Laughter, competition, and fun are usually not key components of the traditional concept—but they can be.

A teachable-moment devotion is based on a fun activity, a few questions, and an applicable Bible verse or passage. They can take as little as 15 minutes or up to 45, depending on the age and interest level of your kids. A few minutes are all you need to make a lasting impression with a planned catalyst.

Here are some good examples of scheduled catalysts for one child or the whole family taken from the book *An Introduction to Family Nights Tool Chest:*

- Put together a jigsaw puzzle with the pieces upside down for a lesson on finishing difficult tasks.
- Give each child a tube of toothpaste and have a race to see who can squeeze the tube empty the fastest, then ask them to put the paste back in. This illustrates that reckless words can't be taken back.

The Battle

Nancy Parker Brummett uses stories to share with her grandchildren the principles of the Christian life. One of her favorites is this gem:

An old Cherokee told his grandson about a fight that was going on between two wolves inside him. "One is evil; it eats anger, envy, sorrow, regret, greed, arrogance, self-pity, guilt, resentment, inferiority, lies, false pride, superiority, and ego," he said. "The other is good; it eats joy, peace, love, hope, serenity, humility, kindness, benevolence, empathy, generosity, truth, compassion, and faith."

The grandson thought about it for a minute and then asked his grandfather, "Which wolf wins?"

The old Cherokee simply replied, "The one I feed."

- A flashlight game can teach a lesson on how the Holy Spirit guides us.
- Milk and a drop of food coloring can show that sin discolors our whole lives.
- A brown paper sack and some everyday objects can teach the lesson that you can't tell from the outside what is inside a person.
- Racing through an obstacle course while holding some building blocks can teach a valuable lesson on responsibility. The more blocks you hold, the more careful you have to be.

Once you've used a planned catalyst to teach a lesson, you can use other spontaneous catalysts to follow up the basic concept.

The Formal Sets Up the Informal

After the family night when Joy was introduced to the subject of peer pressure, I (Jim) was able to have a quick follow-up lesson a few weeks later when a catalyst presented itself. Joy told me that two other girls on her soccer team were Christians, so when we saw a football game where a few players knelt in a prayer of thanksgiving after the game, I asked Joy, "What would it take for you and those other girls to kneel in prayer after your games?" She shrugged. "What's stopping you? Fear of what your friends will think?" And we had another discussion about how the opinions of others shouldn't keep a Christian from honoring God.

She may never pray after a soccer game; that's not my goal, though I'd be pleased if it happened. My goal is to be obedient and teach her, formally and informally, biblical principles, to pray for her, and to do my best to give her a vision for what a dynamic Christian life is all about. How she lives that out is not in my control. What are in my control are those moments when I can teach her in a positive, relevant way what the Bible says about living a life of faith.

Kurt Bruner and his wife, Olivia, also structure their family life so that informal lessons follow a formal lesson about God's truths. One example is a point system on manners. Whenever they go to someone's house, the children have an opportunity to earn points for being polite, respectful, and saying those key words *please* and *thank you*. The children also have an opportunity to lose points—and I'm sure you all know what those behaviors look like. When a Bruner child accumulates enough points, he or she is then given a reward, such as a special toy or an ice cream outing. The system was set up and explained formally so that the concept of respect could be reinforced informally. After an evening out at someone's home, the points are awarded or subtracted, and a teachable moment about good and poor behavior takes place. Because the children are anticipating earning points, they are eager to discuss their behavior and the principles behind their actions.

Prayer Catalysts

Making prayer a habit will provide ways for you to remember and discuss those times when God intervenes for His people. Lisa Donohue prays daily with her daughter, Meghan, who is three years old. She recalls one of Meghan's first answered prayers:

> Meghan wanted to pray for baby Cloe, an infant who attends the same daycare and needed heart surgery. So every night for a week before the operation Meghan prayed, "Jesus, please help Baby Cloe on her surgery for her heart." After the surgery, I told her that God had answered her prayer and that Baby Cloe's heart was all better. That night she still prayed the same prayer out of habit. Once she realized her little mistake, she said, "Thank you, Jesus. Amen."

Making prayer a good habit will provide many instances for rejoicing over God's goodness. Prayer also teaches other valuable lessons that provide catalysts for teachable moments. Warren and Carol Tustin taught their three children a life principle by praying together as a family:

> When my husband and I finally decided to allow our kids to get a dog, we began praying about it with the family. The kids were ages 10, seven and four, and they were really excited to see what kind of dog God was going to provide for us. One Saturday, a pet adoption agency was showing animals at a local pet store, and we went to visit. They had several really cute puppies, but when I asked about the breed, the adoption worker told me the puppies were going to get huge.
>
> We went home puppyless, and I explained that we couldn't get one of those puppies because we needed a dog we could travel with. My family went back the next week, and sure enough, the puppies were still there. But that day, the adoption worker told me about another dog, a small dog, being shown at another location nearby, so we went to check it out.
>
> God had the cutest little Lhasa apso waiting for us. He's been perfect for our family. He can travel with us, and he'll stay small—puppy sized—but he'll always be loved in a big way. Through praying together and waiting, my children have learned that sometimes there are good things out there, like the puppies, that you have to pass up to get God's best, in this case, a Lhasa apso!

When your kids pray, it often sets up a teachable moment. Sheila Seifert tells about an opportunity her sister Beth Naylor experienced:

> One day Beth came upon all three of her girls sitting in the car. Two of them were huddled on the floor praying. "What are you doing?" she asked them.

> Two-year-old Jenny jumped up from the floor and began shouting, "I'm a Christian. I'm a Christian."
>
> Beth gave her a hug and asked, "Why did you become a Christian?"
>
> "Because Riley told me to," Jenny answered. That gave Beth the opportunity she needed to explain what becoming a Christian means.

Prayer journals offer a formal way to set up informal teachable moments. I (Marianne) keep a prayer journal for Danielle called the *Happy Book*. I started it so that I would have a concrete record that God answers Danielle's prayers and that He provides for her even when she doesn't pray for a specific blessing. When she was in preschool, for example, she had her first test of faith. A classmate threw Danielle's stuffed spider onto the roof of the school. Danielle had to wait a whole night and half a day before the janitor was available to retrieve it. She had to trust that God would protect the spider from rain and the elements and that no one would go onto the roof to steal it.

When Danielle is feeling down, we can take out the *Happy Book* and review all the good things God has done for her. I ask her, "Didn't God bring you good Christian friends?" "Didn't He get Daddy a job in town so you wouldn't have to move?" "Didn't he heal your grandmother after her stroke?" Those teachable moments help her put life into a spiritual perspective and remind her that God does care for her. I don't want her hitting those turbulent teenage years without a strong belief that God listens to her personal prayers.

When you pray out loud, you can remind your children of just what prayer is. One Saturday, shortly after a family discussion on worry, I (Jim) tucked my checkbook into my back pocket. My two sons and I climbed into the truck for our weekly trip to the hardware store.

When we got there, I got out of my truck and reached into my pocket—and noticed I didn't have my checkbook anymore. Somehow, somewhere along the way, I had lost it. I said to the kids, "Guys, I messed up. Let's get back in the truck."

The Princess Bride

Do your kids love to laugh? Try a movie catalyst for a teachable moment by renting a video or DVD of the classic comedy *The Princess Bride* and watching it together. Then use the study guide below to put the "parental" back into "Parental Guidance." The material is taken from *Movie Nights* by Bob Smithouser, a must-have resource for any family who enjoys watching movies. Be sure to add the tasty popcorn and special drinks.

Before you watch:

Around the dinner tabletalk about favorite childhood fairy tales. What do many of these stories have in common? In other words, what makes a compelling story?

Chose one or two of these topics for a teachable moment after the movie:

1. What is Westley's attitude toward Buttercup at the beginning of the story? How does his consistent service change her contempt for him into sincere affection? Read Matthew 20:28, Luke 22:26, and Galatians 5:13-14. What example did Jesus set for us in the area of service? Ask these questions: How do we serve each other in our family? Do we ever take each other for granted? What can we do to serve each other better? Aim for specific ideas like "I can take care of the dog in the morning" rather than "I can help more around the house."

2. Early in the story, Grandpa reads, "That day, [Buttercup] was amazed to discover that when [Westley] was saying, 'As you wish,' what he meant was, 'I love you.'" Sometimes parents say "I love you" to their children in

We did. My son Josh said, "Dad, let's pray about it."

I said, "Okay, Josh."

Josh prayed a beautiful prayer that included this request: "God, will You please deliver our checkbook? It's important to us."

ways that are difficult for teens to understand (holding them to a curfew, denying them certain things, building character in ways the teen finds unpleasant, etc.). Talk about this. Help your teen to start hearing "I love you" in the midst of caring, reasonable rules and discipline.

3. What in Westley's attitude makes him a hero? What does he have in common with heroes from other favorite stories, including Bible stories? For teen girls, recall scriptural conquests of Deborah or Esther. (See Judges 4 and the book of Esther.)

4. What does Humperdinck do that makes him a coward? What other flaws make him unworthy? Read Proverbs 8:13, 11:2, and 16:18. How does Humperdinck's arrogance set him up for defeat?

5. Inigo wants to avenge his father's death, and it seems he is satisfied once he kills Count Rugen. See what the Bible has to say about vengeance and justice in Romans 12:19, Acts 17:31, and Hebrews 10:30-31. How can movies manipulate us into rooting for someone like Inigo even when we know his quest is morally misguided?

6. Westley, Inigo, and Fezzik use different strengths (brains, skill, and brawn) to defeat Humperdinck. And they all admit they couldn't have done it alone. What does the Bible say about using our different gifts for God? Read Romans 12:4-8 and 1 Corinthians 12:13-27.

7. In Buttercup's dream, the old peasant woman accuses her of turning her back on Westley's love: "True love saved her in the Fire Swamp, and she treated it like garbage." Read John 1:10-12. How do some people treat Christ's sacrifice with contempt?

—Bob Smithouser

That gave us an opportunity to talk about prayer. What is prayer? How can God answer prayer? What if He says yes, no, or wait?

Two weeks later, I got a package in the mail. I called my kids. I said, "Hey, guys, remember how God said He answers prayer?"

After we reviewed the ways in which He might answer, I held up the checkbook, which had been returned in the package. I said, "This time God was telling us, 'No, not right now.'" We opened up the checkbook, and not a check was missing.

Holiday Catalysts

Holiday traditions are unforgettable. The memories they create waft through the heart like perfume and sweeten the soul. Because traditions are treasured, they make fantastic catalysts for teachable moments.

Here are some ideas for creating spiritual traditions during holidays:

- Halloween: Don't let that jack-o'-lantern frighten you! Jim Weidmann offers a way to turn that pumpkin into a gospel-teaching tool. First, clean out the pumpkin—that gook represents sin. Next, carve a happy face. That's to show the joy in a Christian's life. Last, put a small candle inside, representing the Holy Spirit's presence and the command for us to be light for the world.
- Thanksgiving: At the first Thanksgiving, corn was part of the celebration. Make it part of yours, too. Take a scoop of popcorn kernels and give each family member about six of them. Then pass a plate around the table. When the plate comes to each person, he or she drops a kernel onto the plate and tells about one thing he or she is thankful for. Younger kids may want to glue the corn seeds to a paper plate in the shape of a happy face to represent their joy in knowing that God provides.

- Christmas: Choose among the many Advent celebrations, but be sure to select ones that are meaningful to your child to create the best teachable moments. Buy an inexpensive, unbreakable nativity scene for little ones so they can reenact the Christmas story with the figurines. Older children will be ready to discover and absorb the fact that the little baby in the manger was and is God's Son. Going through the Old Testament prophecies will help bring meaning to His divine birth (a good study Bible will provide a list of them). Teens should be ready to focus on giving rather than receiving during this holiday. Help them discover ways they can share the Good News with their friends. This can be giving symbolic gifts or ornaments with Scripture verses attached, or making sure that friends are offered a ride to a Christmas Eve service if they are willing to attend.
- Easter: There's enough joy and surprise in Jesus' resurrection to keep kids mesmerized for eternity. So forget the bunny, but keep the plastic eggs and fill 12 of them with the following reminders about the events surrounding the Resurrection. Open one egg per day starting 12 days before Easter Sunday. Talk about the contents of each egg and its corresponding Scripture passage. For teens, go ahead and read the text as it is from the Bible. For younger children, you'll have to paraphrase. This activity is designed around John's gospel.
    - John 12:1-11/a piece of cotton with perfume on it.
    - John 12:12-19/some sort of symbol for a palm branch, strips of green paper will do.
    - John 12:20-33/a popcorn kernel or other seed.
    - John 12:34-36/a flashlight bulb or other tiny light bulb.
    - John 13:1-17/a piece of terry cloth towel or a sliver of soap.
    - John 13:18-30/a small piece of bread.
    - John 18:1-11/an olive.

- John 18:12-14, 19-24/a piece of rope or twine.
- John 18:28-40/a piece of paper with a gold crown drawn on it.
- John 19:1-16/a thorn and a piece of purple cloth.
- John 19:17-37/a cross made out of twigs and twine or thread.
- John 19:38-42/strips of white gauze. On Easter Sunday, give your children an empty egg to represent the empty tomb and read John 20:1-23 to them.

Ask your older children to teach their younger siblings so that they learn how to pass on their spiritual legacy.

Younger children will struggle with some of the concepts presented in the holiday traditions. Over time, however, the truths will sink in and be anchored in their hearts. The Bruner children have been using the plastic egg teachable moments for several years. Last year the youngest prayed, "Thank you, Jesus, for dying for the eggs." But Kurt knows the egg tradition works in the long run; the older children know the Easter story so well they are now telling it to the younger children.

You may think these everyday catalysts and the subsequent talks don't make a difference. You may see more spiritual growth after your child goes to a Christian camp or attends a confirmation class, and you're content to wait for those structured teaching events. You may be thinking, *Why bother with teachable moments?* But the evidence that God works through your teaching will one day bear fruit. Lynn Sidebotham, a mother of four sons, put it this way:

> I always wondered if my kids listen, if they apply what I teach them. Is it worth it?

One year my son and I read a book by Mildred D. Taylor, an African American author who writes historical fiction. I used an incident in the book as a teachable moment to illustrate the evils of misusing women sexually and pointed out that the widespread mistreatment of black women is an extremely sad part of American history. The Bible has a lot to say against that kind of selfishness and disrespect.

Not long afterward, my son, who was an eighth-grader at the time, saw a friend leering at a girl in class. My son told the other boy to cut it out. The other boy said something like "As if you never do it," and my son said, "I try not to, because it's wrong."

The lesson had gone beyond what I had expected; I was trying to sensitize my son to treat all women with respect, and he internalized it to such a degree that he has become a champion.

Yes, the effort is worth it!

Truth: The Third Component of a Teachable Moment

Sir Winston Churchill's pithy remark "Men occasionally stumble over the truth, but most of them pick themselves up and hurry off as if nothing ever happened" helps parents understand their role as a mentor. Your children will see non-Christians stumble over God's truth and then ignore it. The world will not listen when the Bible calls them to put others first, to control their sexual appetites, to give and to forgive, to be light, to be holy. The world runs away from those truths. When Christian children find the truth, parents must encourage them to embrace it instead of hurrying off. Christian children must be taught to cling to the biblical principles everyone else scorns.

One of those hard-to-accept truths is "Do not overcome evil by evil, but overcome evil with good" (Romans 12:17). If you diligently teach this truth, your children will be shaped by it. For example, Salli S. enrolled her son in group tennis lessons one summer. The instructor played tennis and power games with equal intensity. He was king of the court and let everyone around him know it. If he didn't like a parent, he asked the parent to leave. If anyone complained, the response was "tough luck." In his tennis game, the score never included "love."

Salli recalls:

> We were already pretty stressed out, and I didn't want this devilish instructor taunting my son. In fact, I was furious that I was paying him to treat us so poorly. But my son, Jay, and I

Teachable Moments Remembered #3

- "My dad and I would read Scripture, usually Proverbs, before I went to school in junior high. This kept me floating during a period when I was lukewarm in my Christian life."
- "During high school, Dad and I would often eat breakfast together at our kitchen table, and we'd sometimes talk about spiritual questions I had. My favorite part, which encouraged me most, was when we ended that time in prayer. It really prepared me for the day."
- "My mom and I had long conversations in her room at night before bed. These 'debriefing' conversations not only allowed me to share my heart and struggles with her, but they also allowed her to give me guidance and the assurance that she was always there to encourage. The culmination of these times—the laughter, tears, and times of conflict—created an impenetrable bond between us."
- "When I made wrong choices, my mother would sit down with me and discuss the situation and conclude with how Jesus would have handled the situation."
- "In middle school, my parents were separated for a while. My mom encouraged my brother and sister and me to memorize a passage to help us through that time. Jeremiah 29:11-14 is still my favorite passage."

decided to see what prayer would do, because I felt strong that it was our duty and that Jay needed to learn that God expects us to return evil with goodness.

I asked Jay if he could be a living example on the tennis court for the instructor to see and show the difference between a real Christian and a phony one. He agreed, even though it meant putting up with kids who were allowed to say, "Ha, ha, you missed your shot" or "I'm not going to return any of your serves because I don't want to play with you." We prayed every day before we started tennis lessons; we specifically prayed for the instructor and that our actions and attitudes would be humble.

In one week the instructor commented on Jay's improved demeanor and asked me a few questions about the Bible. After three weeks, Jay's tennis serve improved markedly, as did his servant attitude.

From this teachable moment, Jay's head knowledge of Scripture was moved down 18 inches to his heart. He has discovered the truth of the Bible's command to return evil with good by living it out.

Put Truth to the Test

When parents who have developed a good relationship with their children recognize a catalyst, they are ready to pair that catalyst with a biblical truth. The third component of a teachable moment is selecting an appropriate truth to teach.

Teachable moments are uniquely appropriate for teaching spiritual principles. All truths are equally true, but they are not equally life-changing. Your children will probably be more interested in learning what Jesus taught about prayer than in knowing that King David appointed Jashobeam the son of Zabdiel to be in charge of more than 24,000 military men (1 Chronicles 27:2).

The information that follows is a list of Bible facts and principles that were adapted and expanded from the *Parents' Guide to the Spiritual Growth of Children,* edited by John Trent, Ph.D., Rick Osborne, and Kurt Bruner. The list includes 112 truths that are broken down into age groups: 0–4, 5–6, 7–9, 10–12, 13–15, and 16–18. Under each age heading are listed the biblical topics/principles that children should be able to grasp during that developmental window. These are guidelines, not laws. Many of the truths are so general that multiple truths can be found within their definitions.

Most of the truths need to be revisited from time to time; to say that a 17-year-old doesn't need to be taught "God created the world" because he learned it in preschool limits the concept. He'll need to be reminded of that fact when he's faced with the theory of evolution on

Jesus' Shadow

Sometimes a teachable moment presents itself, but I'm not sure my children can grasp the truth that goes along with it. I lean toward the side of offering it anyway and pray that God will honor my intentions. Sometimes God takes a lesson I had designed and changes it to meet His designs.

At age three, Justin will steal anything confectionery and hide to eat it. One day he moved a chair to the kitchen counter, climbed on top of it, then reached to the top of the refrigerator and grabbed the brightly colored children's vitamins. After taking the bottle into his bedroom, he opened the "childproof" cap and proceeded to share them with his twin brother, Kendrick. When I found them, Justin was doling out the little pills by the handful, and Kendrick's cheeks were stuffed as full as a chipmunk's. After fishing them out of his mouth, I counted 12 whole and estimated that another three had already turned into vitamin drool.

Other times, Justin runs into the backyard and hides behind the shed to eat a stolen cookie or other sweet. One day, I caught him with some bubble

The Discovery Channel. All Christians need to hear these life-changing truths often. As children age and mature, they will find that the simplest truths are the most profound, and an old truth will touch their lives in new ways. Karl Barth, a famous theologian known for his complex arguments and thoughts, was often asked what was the most profound truth he knew. His answer was "Jesus loves me, this I know, for the Bible tells me so."

Ages 0–4

1. God exists.
2. God loves you.
3. Jesus loves you.
4. God wants to take care of you.

gum and used his guilty look to introduce a teachable moment. I tried to convince him that the weird feeling in his heart was telling him not to take candy. That weird feeling was God, because God is watching him and knows what he's doing even if Mommy doesn't. I knew that the concept of omnipresence was a bit beyond his developmental grasp, and I didn't think he'd learned anything—until my husband bought a new nightlight.

The first night it was in use, the twins were in bed when Kendrick noticed a new shadow on the ceiling. "Look, a balloon!" he said, commenting on the shape.

"No it not," Justin said. "It's Jesus. See His head?"

"A balloon," Kendrick said.

"No, it Jesus." Justin was adamant. "Mommy said He's watching me."

That settled it. To Justin, the shadow was Jesus' presence watching him as he slept. He felt safe and secure knowing the shadow was there. That wasn't the exact lesson application I had in mind, but I'll take it.

—mkh

5. God created everything.
6. God created you.
7. God gave us the Bible.
8. God's Son, Jesus, died for your sins so you can be with God.
9. Prayer is talking to God.
10. You need to talk to God regularly.
11. You need to regularly listen to stories about God and Jesus from the Bible.
12. God wants you to be good, kind, and loving.
13. God wants you to see and think good things.
14. God wants you to go to church.
15. God wants you to obey your parents.
16. God wants you to learn to share your things with others.

Ages 5–6

17. God is your loving heavenly Father. He wants to guide, teach, love, protect, and provide for you.
18. Jesus showed us who God is and what He's like.
19. God is everywhere, He can do anything, and He knows everything.
20. Jesus has always been with God and is God.
21. God tells you about Himself; His Son, Jesus; and His plan for you in the Bible.
22. God sent His Son, Jesus Christ, to die for you.
23. God has prepared a place for you in heaven. Jesus is coming back for you.
24. You can have a relationship with God by accepting what Jesus offers you: salvation.
25. God wants to have a relationship with you.
26. You can talk to God through prayer.
27. You can thank God and Jesus for all the good things in your life.
28. You can ask God for wisdom and guidance.

29. You can read about God and His Son, Jesus, in the Bible or in a Bible storybook.
30. God has a plan for you.
31. The Bible tells you the kind of person God wants you to be.
32. God's way works best. You can be all God wants you to be by following Jesus.
33. God wants you to put only good things into your heart.
34. When you sin, you should ask God to forgive you—and He will.
35. God wants you to spend time with other Christians, both at church and in the community.
36. God wants you to help others and be nice to them.
37. God wants you to obey Him and follow Jesus in everything.
38. God wants you to share and take good care of everything He gives you.
39. God wants you to understand and memorize Bible verses.

Ages 7–9

40. You can be sure that God is real.
41. There is only one God.
42. God exists in three Persons: Father, Son, and Holy Spirit. This is called the Trinity.
43. God is eternal.
44. Jesus is both God and man.
45. Nothing exists apart from God creating it.
46. God's character is true, honest, loving, compassionate, generous, selfless, forgiving, merciful, trustworthy, faithful, just, impartial, and holy.
47. The Bible is true. It is God's Word, and you can trust it.
48. God made sure all stories in the Bible are part of the same larger story.
49. Not everyone obeys God.

50. God wants you to learn and study the Bible.
51. The world is full of sin. There is an enemy in the world (Satan).
52. Jesus died to save you from the penalty for sin.
53. Jesus defeated sin and Satan.
54. Jesus is the only way to God.
55. You read the Bible to learn who God is and what He has done and is doing.
56. You can pray your own prayers or with your parents.
57. Prayer benefits you in many ways.

Honest Abe

When I use teachable moments, I find that God uses the selected truths to refine my heart as well. When Danielle was 10, she read about an episode from Abraham Lincoln's days as a young store clerk. One day he overcharged a customer and walked three miles to the woman's home to give her the correct change.

Danielle was so impressed by Lincoln's action that she talked about it all afternoon. We had a teachable moment and decided that our family should aim to be that honest when it comes to finances. We would do the right thing, even if it became a big inconvenience.

During the next four-week period, I was presented with the following situations:

- Justin took a 25-cent toy car at a garage sale. When we discovered the theft, I made a 40-minute trip to pay for the car.
- During an excursion to a small carnival, the ride attendants kept forgetting to ask for our tickets. Instead of being passive and accepting a free ride, I had to ask them to take our tickets.
- The groceries were loaded, the kids strapped in their car seats. Then I found I had forgotten to pay for the eggs. I returned to the store, waited in line again, and paid for them.

58. Sometimes life gets hard, and you should keep praying because that's the way God makes you stronger.
59. You can trust God and turn your life over to Him.
60. You should learn to seek God.
61. Jesus gives you peace.
62. God wants you to learn and grow and become like Jesus.
63. Growth is a learning process.
64. Your character should match God's character.
65. God wants you to develop your talents.

- When I got my daycare bill, I noticed the invoice was short by six hours, or about $40. I did all sorts of gold-medal-winning mental gymnastics to justify a way to keep the money…1. The twins were sick and hadn't been there all the hours anyway; perhaps this is poetic justice. 2. I hate the daycare's no-cancellation policy—this is payback for all the times the twins couldn't come and they didn't show me mercy. I already lost work time and had to pay for doctor visits and antibiotics; isn't that enough? 4. It was the director's mistake, not mine. If she wants the money, she can do a better job keeping the books.

I waited until the last day to write the check, the last hour actually, and then finally asked the director to correct the bill. She didn't even say thank you, but I could tell she was surprised I had pointed out a $40 error in the daycare's favor.

That first teachable moment with Danielle had turned into an extra-credit assignment for me. I had to admit that old Honest Abe had made an impression on me, too. I'll never know for sure if I would have paid the full daycare bill if I hadn't had honesty on my mind all month. But the fact is, I did. And I know if Danielle has honesty on her mind, she'll make the right choices too.

—mkh

66. God wants you to develop the fruit of the Spirit, which is love, joy, peace, patience, kindness, goodness, faithfulness, gentleness, and self-control (Galatians 5:22).
67. God wants you to mature and develop your personality.
68. Church is God's idea. Jesus is the head of the Church. At church you learn about God and encourage each other to follow Jesus.
69. God wants you to understand what a blessing people and good relationships are.
70. God has taught you right from wrong. He did this to keep you safe and to give you a good life.
71. The Ten Commandments are a good guide for life.
72. God wants you to share your faith.

Ages 10–12

73. Not everyone believes the truth about God, but there are ways you can respond to their objections. (Handling contrary opinions about God, or basic apologetics; you can also study other religions so that you are equipped to handle their questions.)
74. God wants you to explore the Bible.
75. God put the Bible together in a fascinating way. Some dozens of authors over a period of several thousand years created a book with a single, unifying profile of God and His will and purpose.
76. You need to learn how to study the Bible.
77. God lets His people serve Him and worship Him in different ways.
78. God gave us an accurate record of His Son, Jesus.
79. God wants you to tell others about what Jesus has done.
80. Jesus will return as Judge, and there will be a new heaven and a new earth.
81. You can pray on your own.
82. You can read the Bible on your own.

83. You can learn to worship God and Jesus on your own or in a group.
84. God wants you to choose to grow, learn, and seek His wisdom.
85. You don't have to live the Christian life on your own. God is working in you by His Holy Spirit.
86. God wants you to find and follow His will for your life.
87. God wants you to choose to commit your entire life and everything you have to Him.
88. God wants you to choose His way because you love Him and want to be like Jesus.
89. God wants you to learn to seek and follow His Spirit's leading.
90. You need to learn how to resist temptation and Satan.
91. You need to get involved in church and find your place in the body of Christ.

Ages 13–15

92. God is your provider. You can trust him to take care of your financial needs.
93. God is the God of people groups and families. He is also a personal God—your God.
94. God's love is based on His goodness, not on your love-ableness.
95. God is more interested in building your character than He is in making you comfortable. God loves you and helps you, but He doesn't always make things easy.
96. When you have depressing or sad thoughts, God wants you to pray. He will help you.
97. God wants you to pray for your family, friends, your future spouse, your nation, and the world.
98. God wants your words to be wholesome. Cursing or taking the Lord's name in vain is inappropriate. God does not want you to gossip or to tease with harsh jesting.

99. The Bible warns against getting drunk or letting anything control your mind, be it alcohol or drugs.
100. God wants you to witness to people who are different from you. They can be different in their cultural background, how much money they have, their skin color, hobbies, or their taste in music.
101. God wants you to be sexually pure in thought and deed.
102. God wants you to choose friends who will help you become a stronger Christian. Find those friends who ask, "What would Jesus do?"

If Any Mom Lacks Wisdom...

We're PBS people. Network television usually enters our home only for football season, and when it does, I have to prepare myself for the inevitable teachable moments the TV commercials bring. Last year, I had the privilege of explaining why some people enjoy the crude humor of "Make 7-Up Yours" and challenged my family to avoid "coarse jesting" as Ephesians 5:4 admonishes.

But I wasn't ready this year.

How do you explain to a 12-year-old, Hardy Boys loving, hockey-playing boy that the man in the commercial thinks it's alluring to dress up like a French maid before having sex with his girlfriend? And that the old man down the hallway thinks the French maid outfit is sexy instead of ridiculous? Fornication, homosexuality, cross-dressing, sexual fantasy foreplay—those were the underlying concepts of the "humorous" Bud Lite commercial sponsoring a college football game. Why was I not laughing?

We have talked about the Bible's standards for sex. My son knows where babies come from and something about homosexuality and the word

Ages 16–18

103. God has shaped you and designed you for His plans. He is the potter; you are the clay. Your destiny is found in Him.
104. God gives you the strength and resources to face each day, no matter how tough it is.
105. God's purpose for sending Jesus was to offer forgiveness to the world. He will forgive your sins if you ask Him in Jesus' name.
106. God wants you to honor your parents even when it is difficult.
107. You need to choose God as your own God. He does not want lip service to a family tradition; He wants your heart.

lesbian. But because my son would still much rather slug a girl in the arm than kiss her cheek, I don't really think it sank in. He's still very naïve—thank God for that! Because of that naïveté, I haven't gone into the details, especially about homosexuality and cross-dressing. But perhaps I should have covered a bit more ground, because the very next day my son started seventh grade and asked why one of his classmates told him the math teacher is "gay" and then laughed.

We couldn't discuss the issue then, so I've got some time to do some homework and study what the Bible says about sex before I teach my son about it. But where do I start? And, more important, where do I stop? Do I teach him about all the ungodly things people do in the name of sex so he can understand his math teacher's lifestyle and TV commercials? (I can forbid "Monday Night Football," but can I forbid math?) Do I include bestiality? How about necrophilia or group masturbation?

I need wisdom. I'm not going to do a thing until I've studied and prayed and waited. I know God will give me the right timing, the right Bible verses, and the right words. I'll certainly need them.

—anonymous

108. God wants you to live each day for Him and to be prepared to serve Him today with the gifts He has given you. This will help you discover your identity.
109. You need to be learning how to be respectful, honoring, self-sacrificing, and self-controlled. These are the qualities that make a good spouse.
110. God wants you to stand against the common culture. This takes self-control.
111. By discovering your spiritual gifts, you can better serve God and the church. You will be satisfied only when you are serving others with your God-given gifts.
112. Feelings can be deceptive. God wants you to obey Him and renew your mind by reading the Bible so you will not be led astray by emotions or arguments that appeal to your emotions.

Matching the Truth to the Right Moment

Finding a truth that matches a catalyst is not a science; it more resembles good fashion sense. Before selecting the right outfit, you must first check the weather. Do you need a coat or a tank top? Then you need to know where the clothes are going to be worn. Do you need something formal, or will jeans do? Plus, you need to know how strong a fashion statement is required. A fuchsia broomstick skirt or a simple black dress? And finally, does it fit, or will it be uncomfortable after dining at an all-you-can-eat restaurant?

A similar line of thought often takes place when a catalyst confronts you. This process will become automatic once you learn the technique, much like grabbing the right outfit for work. But before you're a natural, first you think through a series of questions: Does this truth match our current mood? Is it appropriate for my child's age level and interests? Can we cover this topic in a few sentences, or do I need a Bible handy for further study? Will my child be mature enough for this truth, or will he or she choke on it? Is there a better truth to go with this moment?

Most of the time these questions are asked and answered intuitively. We don't recommend carrying around a checklist to gauge the appropriateness of certain truths; you do need to practice, however, before your instincts can be refined so that you *know* when and how to present a truth.

When to Let a Moment Pass

Certain fashion faux pas, however, are so bad that they should be avoided if at all possible. For example, no matter how good your figure, a bathing suit is not appropriate attire for a job interview at the FBI, and leave the Darth Vader costume behind at your child's baptism. Teachable moments have the same potential for pitfalls, and you need to watch out. But after a little practice, common sense will prevent you from committing a teachable moment blunder.

Here are some general guidelines. Make sure your child is…

- in a good mood
- well-fed
- able to focus on the conversation
- alert and interested

Sound simple? Well, it's a bit trickier than that, because as a caring parent, your zeal will lead you to pounce on any catalyst that creeps into your territory. And once you get good at spotting catalysts, they'll seem to be everywhere. Consider this example: Have you ever noticed that you can tell a certain kind of wood from its pattern or grain? Pine has knots and swirls, oak has thick stripes that remind you of a tiger. In the same way, we Christians are supposed to have a certain pattern, an identifiable nature that separates us from others.

There's a natural tendency to focus on the great idea rather than your child. You may think chasing the teachable moment catalyst is great fun, but if your child isn't engaged, the message's impact will blend into the scenery and vanish. Too many teachable moments will cause your child to disengage from the message and perhaps even the relationship.

You can use a bad grade on a math test as a catalyst, for example, but you may want to wait until your child has gotten over the initial

Don't Be Blind

Not all teachable moments must be about biblical truths. Passing along life lessons based on pure common sense is also valuable.

Dr. James Dobson recalls a teachable moment when his son, Ryan, was a teen. The two got up early one morning to hunt, which was one of their favorite father-son activities. They situated themselves in a deer blind, and 20 yards away was a feeder that operated on a timer. At 7:00 a.m., it would automatically drop kernels of corn into a pan below, luring unsuspecting deer.

Dr. Dobson picks up the story:

> Ryan and I huddled together in this blind, talking softly about whatever came to mind. Then through the fog, we saw a beautiful doe emerge silently into the clearing. She took nearly 30 minutes to get to the feeder where we were hiding. We had no intention of shooting her, but it was fun to watch this beautiful animal from close range. She was extremely wary, sniffing the air and listening for the sounds of danger. Finally, she inched her way to the feeder, still looking around skittishly as though sensing our presence. Then she ate a quick breakfast and fled.
>
> I whispered to Ryan, "There is something valuable to be learned from what we have just seen. Whenever you come upon a free supply of high-quality corn, unexpectedly provided right there in the middle of the forest, be careful! The people who put it there are probably sitting nearby in a blind, just waiting to take a shot at you. Keep your eyes and ears open!"

disappointment. Or a joyful event, say, winning the state title in a sport, can be something to spark a biblical conversation, but let your child rejoice and enjoy the thrill of victory before expecting him or her to be focused enough to absorb a truth. Jesus fed the five thousand before preaching. He waited until the disciples had been with him through many miracles before he started talking about His death. Timing is everything.

Here's an example of bad timing that happened to me (Marianne). The walk to the public library is one mile from our home—straight uphill. On this particular Saturday, Danielle and I needed to go to the library so she could meet a classmate and work on a group project. And even though Danielle spends hours a day running for the track team, she dreads the uphill hike.

"Do we have to walk?" she asked.

"Yes. I need the exercise."

"Can I run it?"

"Sure, if you want to carry my laptop so I can keep up with you."

Danielle meandered off to gather her books. Wanting the afternoon to be positive, I called down the hallway, "If you hurry, we'll have about an hour before your partner comes, so you can play on one of the library's computers."

"Okay! Let's go!"

All of a sudden, in her new enthusiasm, Danielle became like a sheepdog, nipping at my heels to get me out the door. She found my shoes and socks, and gathered her book bag and library card.

"Danielle," I said, "remember this turnaround of emotions the next time you feel like being a Christian is boring or too hard. It usually means you've lost your vision. You need to step back and focus on what God's done for you, what your future is, and your enthusiasm will return."

I thought it was one of my better analogies, a perfect teachable moment!

But all Danielle said was, "I know"—her standard answer when she's not mentally engaged or is preoccupied with other stuff.

At first, I considered her attitude snitty, and I thought, *She will learn this lesson even if she doesn't want to. I'm going to sit her down and force her to look up some verses.* But then I caught myself: I just got her focused on the prospect of playing her favorite computer game. Why should I expect her to switch mental gears so quickly and focus on this concept? My timing was all wrong. I'll save my analogy for another day.

I picked up my backpack and said, "So, how much money have you made in your online Neopets store this week?" I didn't want to spoil the walk, so I changed the conversation to something pleasant. And with that long, steep walk ahead of us, I knew we'd have an "uphill battle" otherwise.

Other reasons exist to let a teachable moment pass. Perhaps you have your entire family around and the truth you want to impart would best be shared one-on-one. Or maybe you're having such a good time together that you don't want to intrude on the mood. Rely on your instincts for the timing, but if you're not having at least one opportunity a week to pass along a teachable moment, perhaps you need a plan to help create more opportunities.

What Goes in Must Come Out

The truths for a teachable moment come more easily when the parent is in the habit of studying the Bible. If Bible reading is a daily or even a weekly practice, the Word of God is already on your mind, and those truths are gathered much more quickly.

If you need to brush up on some of those long-forgotten verses or are experiencing Bible study for the first time, two great places to glean practical wisdom quickly are the Gospels and Proverbs. The Sermon on the Mount is in Matthew 5–7; the book of Luke has some interesting parables with profound truths in chapters 10–21; and you'll want to reread the story of the Passion from John's perspective starting with the Lord's Supper in chapter 13 and ending at 21. That's a total of 33 chapters. If you read one chapter a day, in about a month you can give yourself a refresher course on the life of Christ.

The Proverbs are also conveniently sectioned into bite-sized chunks, and there are 31 chapters. Reading one chapter a day will literally give you the wisdom of Solomon!

Here's a teachable moment by Albert Yeh, a senior scientist at a technology firm and father of three, based on a truth found in the Sermon on the Mount (Matthew 5:14-16):

> Five-year-old Moriah wanted to know how a light bulb worked one day while I was replacing a burnt-out bulb. I took out a clear 60-watt light bulb and showed her the filament connected by the two electrodes. When the light bulb is connected to the electrical outlet, electricity flows through the filament, and the filament gives off light. When the filament is broken, no light shines.
>
> I explained to my daughter that we, as Christians, are like light bulbs. God is like the electrical outlet that allows us to shine like a light bulb if we follow His desires.
>
> If we disobey God's words, then we would be like a broken filament that cannot shine in the world.

To find help understanding the Scriptures, I (Jim) recommend reading the *Life Application Bible.* You can read a page a day and take hold of new spiritual concepts through the commentary. It's efficient, effective, and interesting. By taking this simple step, you'll increase your knowledge and be able to offer better bait to your kids so they get hooked on your teachable moments. A truism exists based on Isaiah 55:11: "[My word] will not return to me empty, but will accomplish what I desire and achieve the purpose for which I sent it." You'll find that when you are studying the Bible, even in bite-sized chunks, there will be several opportunities for you to apply it that very day.

Since my son Joshua wants to be a pastor, we have teachable moments about leadership. I recently began reading E.M. Bounds's *On Prayer* and have found that God's chosen leaders are men who pray. I pass along those biblical examples to Josh, knowing that he needs to learn to protect his prayer life to know God's will.

Truth Leaves You Thirsty for More

Have you ever noticed that ice cream makes you thirsty?

Check out your local ice cream shop. It's a good bet there's a drinking fountain. Even though ice cream is cool, sweet, and slides down your throat, it leaves you craving water.

In the same way, a satisfying teachable moment can create a thirst for more truth. I (Jim) recall a teachable moment that led naturally into a Bible study. When my kids were 12, 10, and 8, they attended a home school co-op. One day, when I came home from work, I asked, "Well, what did you guys do in school today?"

They told me that their teacher asked the students to write down all the things they feared.

"Well, what was the outcome?" I asked.

"Dad, it was really interesting," Josh answered. "The number-one thing kids feared was God! The number-two thing was their dad."

I quickly jumped in on that comment to say, "Hey, you don't fear me, do you?"

"Aw, Dad, we didn't put that down. That's what most of the kids put down," Joshua answered for the family.

"Let's talk about this fear of God. How did you guys feel about that? Do you fear God?" I said.

The hemming and hawing stopped when they finally admitted they were a little concerned about God punishing them.

"Then here's what I want you to do..." I said and outlined our plan of action. We went to the back of a study Bible and looked up the word *fear* in the concordance. After reading the passages, we learned that fear should really be an awe-inspired humbleness, not a fear of retaliation. We fear God because we love Him and don't want to mess up in front of Him, not because we're afraid of a lightning bolt or some other bad thing happening to us.

Now that my children know fear, they have no fear!

Speaking of Fear

Truths we share with our children through teachable moments can allay their fears. Beth Naylor remembers when her daughter, five-year-old Molly, received her first Bible:

> Molly began having nightmares. One night, she started screaming in her sleep, "No! No! Stop it!"
>
> I went into her room and slowly tried to wake her. When a groggy Molly finally woke up, I asked, "Honey, what were you dreaming about?"
>
> With fear in her eyes, Molly said, "A teacher was making me read my Bible, and I don't know how to read yet." This gave me the opportunity to let Molly know that God does not require more from us than He has given us the ability to do.

Even when kids are ready to leave home, they still need guidance to help them deal with their anxieties. Doreen Olson, a pastor's wife, mother of two, and executive minister of Christian formation for a mid-sized denomination, remembers her daughter's struggle with choosing a college.

I could tell Kjerstin [Share-stin] was full of angst. She had listed the pros and cons for each of two schools she was considering. That listing didn't help; in fact, she was stymied. The acceptance deadline for each school was rapidly approaching. When I asked her what she felt God wanted her to do, she burst into tears. "I think God wants me to attend the school I least want to go to!"

Is that the image of God we've given her? I thought. "Why would a loving and gracious God deprive one of His children of the desires of her heart?" I asked. "Unless you were headed in harm's way, I don't think God's nature would be constantly looking for ways to restrict our enjoyment of life." We then talked about God's character and His will.

What a relief it was for my daughter to know that God is more interested in a relationship with her than anything else. I told her there have been times when God has indicated that either of two paths I was considering was fine, as long as I stayed close to Him. Kjerstin was elated to be free to choose the college she was really excited about attending.

Church Truth

Curriculum developers want to reach people from the cradle to the grave. A church can even purchase Sunday school take-homes for newborns. But the call in Deuteronomy 6:6 is for parents, not Sunday school teachers, to train their children. Many parents, however, seem comfortable leaving the teaching responsibility with the church.

Here's why that hands-off attitude isn't the best for your children: You can't expect your Sunday school teacher to have a close relationship with a dozen-plus kids. No matter how much fun or gifted a teacher is, that person does not have the commitment level or personal history to understand your child the way you do. The Sunday school teacher has no way of gauging the impact of the lesson. You do. Additionally, a current trend among Sunday school curriculum developers is to create material for a classroom that has rotating teachers. The *GodPrints* curriculum published by Cook Communications Ministries, for example, is designed for more than one teacher, because, especially in large churches, parents can't expect the same adults to be there week to week.

Because of the lack of relationship, the teachable moments that occur during the Sunday school hour can't have the same impact that yours can. The minutes you spend with your child in the car after church can be the most valuable teaching that occurs on Sunday morning.

Debbie Faber, a mother of four, relates this story:

> Lexie is nine and a half years old. She's at that stage where she is no longer just gathering information about God; she's got to have it make sense; it's got to fit into her practical worldview. On the drive home from church last week, I asked what she learned in Sunday school. She told me it was the Creation story. Suddenly we were having an in-depth discussion on the reason people are on the earth. "Why were we even created, Mom?" she asked. "There's got to be a reason."
>
> The discussion covered the purpose for our lives—to live out a calling and please God, to glorify God—all this in terms that she could understand.

Sunday school is great, but sometimes kids leave with more questions than answers. It's up to parents to fill in the blanks.

Should you pull your child from Sunday school? May it never be! Sunday school is valuable, especially when parents take the initiative to follow up on the weekly lesson. The same can be said for youth group. The leaders are usually genuinely concerned about how many kids?

Ten? Twenty? More than a hundred? Jesus himself chose only 12, and they lived together during His ministry so that He could have maximum impact. While most youth pastors are a positive influence, they have limited time and emotional resources; they can't reach all the kids on a personal level.

One way to use youth group time as a catalyst for home teachable moments is to keep in touch with the church youth workers. When you find out what topics the leaders have planned, be sure you cover them yourself—preferably before the youth pastor does. In my life before the twins, I (Marianne) was a youth volunteer for an extremely organized church. The church council had created a list of topics for the youth pastor to cover, and he gave me the job of teaching

Special Delivery

It's amazing what God will do when children seek Him sincerely. We had recently moved overseas to Austria, and my son, Stefan, was seven years old. One morning he observed his older sister, Emilie, reading her Bible at the breakfast table before school; it was the Bible she had received at our home church in Pasadena, California. While Stefan had several Bible storybooks, he didn't have a "real" Bible, and he wanted one like Emilie's. He felt he was old enough for his own, and I agreed. "You will probably get one the next time we go back to California," I reassured him. Off he went to school.

That very afternoon a package arrived in the mail from the children's minister at our home church. They had recently presented all the first-graders with Bibles in a Sunday morning ceremony, and she decided to mail Stefan one too. It was just like Emilie's. We've all been impressed by God's timing—and Stefan has an increased respect for his Bible because it was a special delivery from God.

—Becky Foster Still

the middle school girls about sexually transmitted diseases *on the first night I volunteered!* Most of those girls barely knew my name, and they knew even less about chlamydia. The lesson was awkward, to say the least. I'm sure if the mothers had known what I was going to be talking about, they would have wanted to discuss it with their daughters first. I stole a privilege that belonged to those moms, and I didn't even realize it—and neither did they. Looking back, I wish I had refused to teach the lesson and taken the girls out for Slurpees instead. (More about teachable moments and coming of age is covered in chapter 9.)

If parents take the lead role, however, church programming can be an excellent catalyst for teachable moments. Doreen Olson recalls a church program that affected her family:

> During the weeks before Thanksgiving, we often talked about the many reasons we have to be thankful. We'd discuss Jesus' attitude toward the poor and what God expects of us with regard to sharing what we have. A particularly memorable learning avenue was provided by our church and its partnership with World Relief. Instructions accompanying an offering collected in a soup-can container guided us to give according to what we had been given. Every evening as we gathered for dinner, our two children, ages nine and 12, learned something about the world's poor. For example, we learned that a large percentage of the world's population goes without adequate heat on very cold days. My children dropped 68 nickels into the can, one nickel for each degree of heat registered on our thermostat. Another day we counted all our blankets and made a donation for those, too. These activities motivated Aaron and Kjerstin to learn about children who were less fortunate; I watched them become more generous through these creative family activities.

Actions Speak Louder Than Words

Jim Weidmann often quotes Proverbs 20:11: "Even a child is known by his actions, by whether his conduct is pure and right." Watchful parents can observe their children's behavior and know which truths a child has absorbed and which ones he or she still needs to learn. The famous thinker and scientist Galileo summed up another aspect of truth training when he said, "All truths are easy to understand once they are discovered; the point is to discover them." Many "churched" kids walk away from biblical truths because, while they know all the stories, they have not "discovered" life-changing truth. Biblical truth can be understood and cherished only when it is lived out in faith or discovered in the science lab of life. Teachable moments offer parents a way to help kids discover truth and understand what Jesus has to offer them.

CHAPTER EIGHT

The Challenge and Privilege of Being Vulnerable

Karie Hughes knows all about vulnerability and forgiveness. Feeling lonely and depressed after her divorce, she went to a nightclub, met a guy, and had a one-night stand. That one night lead to months of guilt and shame as she carried an unwanted pregnancy to term and gave the baby up for adoption. Her two children, then ages four and seven, were wide-eyed witnesses to her pain.

To restore her credibility as a Christian with her children, she not only confessed to God and to them but she also became a counselor at a Christian family care agency, helping women in similar circumstances by sharing her experience of God's forgiveness. Currently, she speaks to groups of teens nationwide about sexual abstinence and the biblical standards for purity through an organization she founded: Passion and Principles.

Through her message, she tells about the redeeming power of Christ's love, His forgiveness, and the promise in Romans 8:28 that "in all things God works for the good of those who love him, who have been called according to his purpose." She doesn't encourage her children to be like her; she encourages everyone to be like Christ.

If Karie hadn't been so honest, vulnerable, and visibly changed, her children would be able to accuse her of being a hypocrite and leave the faith. They would have an excuse to sin in the same way. But because her faults have been covered up by the faultlessness of Jesus, her relationship with her kids is strong.

"But the shame never leaves," she reminds us. "There I am, standing up in front of hundreds of kids sharing my story, but all I can think of is my own two children, sitting somewhere in the back at the book table, listening. I wish they didn't have to know."

Karie's sin became exposed because of her pregnancy. But not all past sins can be detected on the surface so easily. What about those past or private sins we all have, the ones that no one else besides God would ever find out if we didn't share them? Why would we tell our own kids that we used illegal drugs, were responsible for an abortion, dodged the draft, or cheated on a standardized exam? What makes it worth it? There may come a time when you feel your teen could benefit spiritually from knowing about your past sins or painful experiences. Talking about your past can be a teachable moment with a torpedo-like impact. But how can you make sure that the impact is positive? When, should, and how do you tell your kids about drug abuse, sexual impurity, or other ungodly or illegal activity? Tim Sanford, a licensed professional counselor, offers these general guidelines before presenting potentially harmful information to your older children or teens:

1. Deal with your past sins or traumatic experiences before discussing them with your child. You must be at spiritual and emotional peace before talking with your teen or older child.

2. What you say, and when you say it, must always be for your child's benefit, not your benefit. Do not do this to relieve your anxiety,

anger, need to vent, desire to get back at your ex-spouse or cleanse your conscience.

3. Always tell the truth; never lie. You may decline to say something or withhold graphic information, but don't whitewash the events. If children catch you in one lie, they will wonder what else you've been lying about.

4. If the details are unsavory, give only enough of them to get your desired point across. If your children press you for more information, simply decline by saying something like "The details aren't the point here; what is important is that by making bad choices, I put myself and others at risk."

5. Teens usually are mature enough to handle the information and would prefer to hear it from you, not indirectly. If you fear that at the upcoming reunion Aunt Sophie is going to tell your sons or daughters about your "partying days," better they hear it first from you. The added benefit is that you're on the offensive against sin, not defending your reputation.

6. Talk with them when you have time to talk it through completely. Don't rush the time or "just slip it in" somewhere. If you're caught off guard by a question, give yourself time to think what the wisest answer is. You may even want to ask your spouse for support or guidance and pray before broaching the subject. That's fine; tell your child something like "That's a good question, and you deserve the best answer I can give. I need to think about it first."

7. Give them the chance to ask questions, and be as honest as you can if and when they do ask.

8. Share with them the journey from "mistake" to "healing" as well. They need to see and hear more than just the outline of the account and the happily-ever-after ending; they need to understand God's grace through the process.

Being honest means you may have to answer some pretty embarrassing questions. When my (Jim's) oldest son was five, he asked about sex, and the questions haven't stopped. Janet and I have been boldly confronted by our kids on why exactly they should wait to have sex. Now as a parent, I can declare, "I want to answer your question, but at the appropriate time and in the appropriate context. But I will answer it."

Each of us needs a place to be open, to reveal intimate details and

Road Test

One day I pulled into a parking lot, and a woman got out of her car and started yelling at me. Her irrational intensity and abusive anger left me dazed. The only thing I could decipher from her ranting was that I had run her off the road and almost killed her. Angry myself now, I said I didn't know what she was talking about, and she stalked off and drove away.

It was nearly 45 minutes later, when my senses were back in order, that I realized what had occurred. I had made a driving mistake; I thought I was in a single left-hand turn lane, when in fact the intersection had a double left-hand turn lane. I had turned and moved into the right-hand lane, effectively and illegally cutting off the woman.

When I got home, I decided to use my mistake for a teachable moment. Retelling the event taught my 17-year-old son, Peter, that even experienced drivers make errors and to always drive defensively, especially in left-hand turn situations. And then we discussed the woman's anger. Her emotions had so overwhelmed me that I couldn't think straight. I would have apologized if she had rationally explained my error. We could have parted in some semblance of peace, but her anger denied me three things: first, clear information; second, a chance to share my view; and third, an opportunity to restore the relationship.

This turn of events, while unfortunate, provided a perfect example to show my son how anger, even righteous anger, can ruin any chance of reconciliation when it is not tempered by self-control.

—Lynn Sidebotham

emotions that no one else will hear. You need to make sure that you can keep your children's secrets and respect their privacy. During these times of honesty you can come alongside and guide, encourage, and bring spiritual light to the situation. Your rule should be Ephesians 4:29, "Do not let any unwholesome talk come out of your mouths, but only what is helpful for building others up according to their needs, that it may benefit those who *listen* [emphasis added]."

Jim Weidmann recommends that parents evaluate the emotional, social, and spiritual maturity of their child before talking about mistakes they have made. Especially in the area of sexual impurity or abortion, it is best to wait until your older teen can handle that type of discussion and deal with it responsibly and confidentially. Sensitive issues should be shared one-on-one, perhaps when you are on a trip alone together. It takes time for children to digest such information, and you want to be there and focused on them while they are processing the painful or disappointing news. Along with the consequences of the mistake, you need to teach that knowledge has responsibility. If there is a chance your children will use the information as an excuse to say, "Mom (or Dad) did it, and she turned out okay," wait, or point out clearly that "okay" is not what God wants for them. God wants the best.

True Confessions?

The details of your sin life shouldn't be up for public display. The goal of sharing is not to rival the content of a primetime talk show and impress your kids with the extent of your evil escapades. But under the right circumstances, it can be helpful to explain to your kids through a teachable moment that you've been down those forbidden roads and the way is painful. You can use those memories to create a teachable moment.

For example, a father of five named Barney recalls an episode in his teens when he wanted to show off in front of a friend, so he walked out of Sears with a $40 electric car set. The boys took the stolen car set to the friend's house, where they had to lie about its origin. After playing with it for a couple of hours, the thrill was gone. Two years later, when Barney was in college, he still felt guilty and knew that God wanted him to make restitution. He called his father and told him what he had done. Together they went to Sears and talked to the security officer. After paying for the cars, Barney had a chance to tell the officer why he had returned after so long: "I'm a Christian and couldn't feel good until I had made things right."

While Barney doesn't share all the details with his children in one sitting, he does let them know that when they do things wrong, guilt and shame will follow them. He also tells them how great it felt to make good his bad action, to have a clear conscience again. And last, he talks with them from experience that confessing and receiving God's forgiveness is real.

When Crises Come Calling

When she was in kindergarten, Rachael Gemmen realized she didn't look like the rest of her family—her skin is dark, her parents' and brothers' skin is light. She asked questions like "Mommy, why am I not white like the rest of my family?" "Am I adopted?" and "When will I become white?"

Rachael was conceived when her mother, Heather, was raped by a stranger. What do you tell a child conceived under those violent circumstances? And when do you tell it?

Heather wished to spare Rachael knowledge of the painful way her life had begun, but answers to Rachael's questions could be found only in the truth. Heather and her husband, Steve, waited until Rachael expressed curiosity before sharing the honest yet simple answers. They told their daughter only what she needed to know and reassured her that her family and God love her, that her place in the family is secure. "Someone else put you in my tummy," Heather said, "but Daddy is your real dad. We're so glad that God picked you out for us." They also affirmed her beauty, helping her to celebrate her brown skin and curly hair.

Bad memories still bring Heather emotional pain. She was, however, able to eclipse the negative memories with the current joy of having a daughter, making conversations about the subject relatively comfortable. Heather hopes that the trusting and loving relationship they have developed will help her daughter to safely understand the facts, even after Rachael is old enough to truly comprehend what rape is.

Jeff Leeland also encourages parents who have suffered or are in crisis to talk about it without undo emotionalism. Sure, you can show concern, grief, and sadness, but panic or desperation can devastate a young child. When a parent is out of emotional control, the child's world is unstable and frightening. During the period his son Michael was in the danger zone because of his leukemia, Jeff and his wife, Kristi, kept a positive, hopeful attitude through prayer. By exhibiting peace, they kept the family atmosphere calm, and their other three children didn't experience a great deal of anxiety. The message the Leeland kids got was "If Mom and Dad trust God, then I can too."

By approaching potentially devastating circumstances with God's peace, you tell your children that He's in control. This creates trust between you and your children, and when they come to you with other problems, they'll know you won't overreact because you have "the peace of God, which transcends all understanding" (Philippians 4:7). They will also know that they won't be overburdening you, because they've seen you "cast all your anxiety on him" (1 Peter 5:7).

Heather and Jeff were made vulnerable by their lives' circumstances, and their children benefited from the honest and loving talks they had with their parents. Because of those discussions, their children trust God more and have a closer parent-child relationship. Heather's crisis has blessed her family in unexpected ways. "My kids can ask me anything," she says. "My friends are amazed at the questions my kids ask with openness. After having talked to them about the rape, there's nothing we can't talk about. Even better than that, each of my kids knows they are handpicked by God to be part of our family. What could give them more security than that?"

Jeff also knows kids need a model to follow when they process pain. "Pain is not the enemy," he says. "It's how you use it. Pain can lead you to God as a healer and source of comfort. It can also teach you to find hope beyond the present moment. By sharing through the pain, parents can point their children to God's higher purpose."

Accountability

I (Jim) was planning to run errands one day with little Jacob beside me in the car. As was my habit, I clicked the garage door opener and rolled the car out of the garage. The car sounded *BAM!* My mouth sounded *"D***!"* as I realized I had smashed the car into the lowering automatic door, splintering it to pieces.

I looked at Jake, and his pupils were big as planets. He stared back at me as if I were an alien. With one angry word, I had destroyed my father-hero image in his seven-year-old eyes. My reputation had come crashing down along with the garage door. And like that door, my heart was in splinters. If I'd had the choice to instantly restore the garage door or my former image in Jacob's mind, I would have chosen to restore our relationship. But how could I?

I let down my son that day, but I didn't let the incident go as if nothing had happened. I had an apology teachable moment and with renewed passion pursued being the best role model I could be. Though I had cracked my father-hero image, it could be mended. In fact, with God's blessing, our relationship became closer because of the apology. When parents become vulnerable through teachable moments and set aside their parental power, children's hearts open up. If you don't acknowledge your errors, however, their hearts will close.

As children grow older, they spot our inconsistencies, failures, and, yes, our sins. They notice when we speed on the freeway, gossip about the choir director, gather credit card debt, tell those white lies to avoid driving the carpool, read lust-filled novels, snap at the grocery store clerk, and lie about the toddler's age to get a free ticket on an airline. And the more of the Bible they know, the more easily they spot our moral frailties. You must acknowledge and apologize for your failures.

When your children are old enough to know right from wrong, they are old enough to help keep you accountable for your actions. As soon as children can read the speedometer and know what a speed limit sign is, they are ready to be your backseat police officers. James

Sharing the Struggle

During a difficult time in my life as a Christian, I wrote a note to my daughter about my struggles and questions. This would, on the surface, seem stupid, since my daughter was seriously questioning her own faith. Wouldn't it be smarter to keep silent on those issues? Might I blow her fragile faith right out of the water?

Don't ask me why I sent her a three-page journal of my struggle, but I did. Her note in response took me by surprise:

I am so honored that you would share something like this with me. It amazes me that we can have this kind of relationship where you feel okay in sharing something so personal.... Here I am, in the throes of questioning all the areas of my faith, and hearing your struggles with yours only makes me feel stronger in mine.... I've often told people that if I could model my faith after anyone, it would be you. Thank you for that.

—Lissa Johnson

Werning, a father of four, gives his children permission to ask, "Daddy, how fast are you going?" whenever they are in the car. That's their way of saying, "Slow down, you're speeding!" After all, their lives are in his hands. It also gives them a chance to see how to accept criticism when James doesn't argue but, instead, slows the car down.

After a family night on the subject of coveting, my (Jim's) wife and children were driving in the car together. Going through the neighborhoods in south Denver can dazzle the eyes. The houses are new and large—and expensive. Upon seeing them, my wife, Janet, was caught up in their beauty and said, "Look at those. Think of all the room we'd have if we could buy one. Everything would be new."

"Mom!" the children exploded. "You're not supposed to covet your neighbor's house!"

With humility, Janet conceded that she had been wrong. That acknowledgment told the children two things. First, adults should follow the rules in the Bible too, and second, we all need reminders to stay focused on God's laws.

I (Marianne) used to consider all the chocolate that enters our house my personal property. It didn't matter who brought it in or where it was hidden—it was mine. It's been that way ever since my daughter, Danielle, was young. I just cleared out her Easter basket or party favor bags of anything brown and yummy. She could keep the suckers and jawbreakers, the jellybeans and Jujube's, but the chocolate was mine. Now that she's older, she doesn't see things my way. She calls that stealing.

Hmmm, I guess that's why it's called stealing candy from a baby. But I know how she feels, because I get pretty upset when Justin finds the M&M's in the van's glove box and the only thing left besides the bag is the brown-and-red drool on his chin. So I've reformed, but I admit, old habits die hard. I'm only about 90 percent reliable if I accidentally find a Hershey's Kiss in her sock drawer or a Kit Kat bar in her backpack.

Because I'm a repeat offender, Danielle's disappointment in me is huge, even if I've gone several months with a clean parole record and I take just an itsy-bitsy, teeny-weeny Tootsie Roll. The teachable moments we've had concerning these incidents have been painful. When Danielle asks, "How can you do that again?" I can tell it's a soul hurt that even a whole box of Godiva chocolates won't appease. Because we have a zero-tolerance policy for stealing at our house and she is the only person who can catch me at my thievery, it's put me in an awkward spot. The child is enforcing the rules, and I hate that. But it's better than stiff-necked denial, because that would create a total breach in our relationship.

As a result of my readiness to admit my fault when my daughter holds me accountable, we now have the language and a history to talk about sin. She believes me when I tell her not to start bad habits, even little ones, because they are so difficult to break and can wear down another person's trust. At least she has hope that I've repented because it's been a long time since I've snitched any chocolate, and I haven't raided this year's harvest party stash. But I don't think her hope is in me—that would be foolish, and my girl is no fool. Her hope is in my other addiction—God. She knows that I "steal away" to talk to Him in prayer.

The other day, some candy was missing from her bureau, and she accused me of taking it. I truthfully said that I hadn't, and she believed me, but perhaps not solely because of my newfound virtue. It probably also has a little to do with the fact that Justin has figured out how to open her bureau drawers.

Empathy Encourages

To encourage, you need to understand where your kids are emotionally. Every child is different. You have to be sensitive to different personalities and make sure you know what's going on emotionally with a particular child. What energizes one will break the spirit of the other. To encourage them with empathy, you have to know how to read them, and sometimes you fail.

When you are able to offer empathy to your child, you are sensitized to his or her feelings, and you know when to be strong, when to share, when to speak those hard truths, and when to simply listen. You increase teachable moments a hundredfold when you can listen with your ears and your heart.

When I (Marianne) was young, my father had tears in his eyes when he told me that my pet quail's head had been bitten off by a neighbor's dog. Those tears were something, because Daddy really didn't like the bird. It was stupid, ugly, and made a mess out of my room and the backyard; he often called it "bird brain." He let me sob away the afternoon, however, never mentioning the fact that now we wouldn't have bird dung all over the place. Neither did he remind me that I never played with the quail anymore anyway. Those tears were something special, because they let me know he remembered what it was like to be a kid and suffer a loss.

Tomato Soup

"Taste this," Jolene, my teenage daughter, said. She held a spoonful of chili to my mouth.

I accepted the spoon, tasting the flavors. At 16, Jolene cooks better than I do. She had used her own recipe. I couldn't identify one of her ingredients, but it had a familiar flavor. "I like it," I told her, spooning piping-hot chili into a bowl. I added cheddar cheese and let the food melt in my mouth. I finally identified the unknown ingredient. "Tomato soup," I said.

"What?"

"I can taste the tomato soup." Seeing the stricken look on her face, I hurried to add, "But it's very good."

Since Jolene knows I hate tomato soup, she suspected I was lying, despite my previous sincere compliments. While Jolene picked at her food, I ate mine with obvious relish, trying to convince her that it was fine.

Another time, I saw what happened when he forgot what it's like to be young. One day, my five-year-old niece lost a plastic dime-store necklace, and she was whining about it. In an effort to get her to emotionally move on he said, "If that's the worst thing that happens to you in life, you'll be lucky." Not appreciating the wisdom of his counsel, she burst into tears and fled from the room.

How and when do you choose to reach out and offer emotional support and empathy? When do you give a "it's time to lift your chin up and get ready for the next fight" speech?

Stroll Down Memory Lane

To start the process of evaluating how to respond in emotional circumstances, recall when you were your child's age and try answering these questions in your mind or on paper:

"I can't believe you said tomato soup," she said with a pout. "You don't like anything with tomato soup in it."

"That's not true! Look at my bowl." I showed her the scraped sides.

"I can't believe you said tomato soup," she repeated.

By then I didn't want to hear any more. "Stop jabbering. I'm tired."

That lit the fire. Jolene yelled at me. I yelled back. In a lull, God spoke. Remember Me? All the words died in my throat.

"Jolene," I said. "I screwed up. We should kneel down right here and ask God to forgive us—and I need to ask you to forgive me."

She looked at me with a surprised expression, then sank to her knees on the cold linoleum floor. With arms locked around each other, we prayed. Forgiveness replaced anger.

Neither Jolene nor I will ever eat tomato soup again without remembering.

—Darlene Franklin

- When you were your child's age, who did you wish you were?
- Who did you hope to become?
- What were your deepest hurts? How did they feel?
- What did you usually do when faced with a crisis?
- How did you feel when your friends were involved in something that you knew wasn't right? What did you do?
- What did you do when someone yelled at you?
- Which of your teachers intimidated you? Why?
- Who was the person you felt closest to?

Once you've gone back in time and remembered what it felt like to be your child's age, ask some questions to make sure you understand the whole story: "What's wrong?" "What happened?" "What are you feeling right now?" "I remember feeling scared. Was that what you felt?"

One time I (Marianne) goofed when Danielle's pet mouse died. The pet, Reepicheep, had been her reward for getting straight A's in fifth grade. I remembered how much my father's empathy meant to me when my bird was eaten, and I tried to reach out in a similar manner by writing her a poem about grief. But Danielle wasn't sad that the mouse had died—she was mad that he had let her down! All my poetic empathy was wasted because I didn't ask what she was feeling.

At other times I can nail what she's experiencing. I've seen half a dozen soccer coaches try to work with her on the field, and they forget to acknowledge her emotions. When she gets hurt in a game and asks to come out, it's useless for a coach to tell her, "It was nothing" or "If you were tough, you'd get back out there." With Danielle (and most kids) you first have to acknowledge that her pain is real. A simple "that sure was a bad spill you took; I bet it hurt" is all she needs to respond, "Yeah, it hurt, but I'm ready to go back out."

To find out how good you are at responding with empathy, take this little test:

You knock on your 13-year-old daughter's bedroom door. You hear a choked "Come in," and you can tell she's crying. When you walk inside, you see a small pile of dark hair on her dresser with scissors next to it. She's lying face down on the bed, her head covered by a quilt. For about five minutes, she won't let you see her face. When she finally raises her head, you notice that she has tried to cut out her widow's peak, a small arrow of hair at her hairline. You say…

a. *So what if your hair will take some time to grow out? You're young. No one will notice, and if they do, they'll forget all about it by high school, and that's when looks really matter.*

b. *Sweetheart, I can see that you've been working on your hair. I hated mine when I was your age; that's when perms were in. A girlfriend tried to give me one, and all it did was frizz my hair. I felt like the Bride of Frankenstein.*

c. *You're lucky! I know just the store. They have these cute little headbands you can wear. It'll cover up that little area, and no one will see it. Who knows? You may even start a new fashion trend.*

d. *Wow, what happened? Are you trying to rival Harry Potter with that scar on your forehead?*

e. *I never would have done that when I was your age. I didn't even care about my hair until I was older. What on earth made you do this?*

Answer *b* is the only answer that gives you a platform to comfort, guide, and walk alongside your child through this emotional time. With answer *b* you won't be blamed with "You don't understand."

While answer *a* may be true, it doesn't meet her at her current emotional level. She's not ready to look even five minutes into the future, let alone high school.

Answer *c* may be part of the right answer after the crisis has passed. Your daughter will need time to adjust and come up with a plan, but she should think of it on her own; that way, if it doesn't work out, she can't blame you. Coming in as the "great parent problem solver" does two things: (1) It says to your teen, "You can't do this on your own," and (2) it takes away an opportunity for your child to grow through failure and take full responsibility for her actions.

Answer *d* might be what you are thinking, but don't utter those words out loud unless you want your daughter to lock herself in the bathroom for six years. Your daughters will remember every negative comment you make about their appearance well into their eighties, forgetting only when they begin to suffer from some sort of dementia. Perhaps a little bit of humor might ease the tension in a few days, but at the crisis moment, only questions and empathy are appropriate.

The last answer, *e*, exemplifies a common pitfall parents often get trapped in. When establishing empathy, you need to prove you can understand your child even if you can't immediately identify with the problem. You need to help your child recognize factors of commonal-

Field of Nightmares

There are vast fields near our home that are vastly attractive to rattlesnakes, and while we live in a good neighborhood, our city has its share of another type of predator—those who seek children. One day, I came home from work and expected to find my son, Matt, home from middle school. No boy, no phone message, no note—where was he? I called my husband, who planned to leave work immediately to help look for him. Just as I was getting into my car to search, a neighbor drove by and said she had seen Matt strolling toward home. I found him and told him to get in the car. After I had a chance to cool down, I explained how frightened I had been, imagining all kinds of awful things that could have happened. Then I was able to explain that just after my eighth-grade year, I had been grounded for the entire summer because I had left one night with friends and not told anyone where I was going.

From Matt's perspective, he had just gone out on a walk and got lost, never thinking that the incident would scare his parents. By telling him that I had been just like him, he was willing to communicate.

—Beth Weeden

ity, not differentiation. So even if you've never ruined your hair, you could tell about some other embarrassing moment, and fortunately, most parents have plenty of those to share.

Showing your kids that you know what they are going through gives hope to even a young child. Ray F., a father of four, recently had an opportunity to share and pray with his six-year-old son, Joseph. Here's his story:

> Joseph was having nightmares every night, and I told him that the same thing happened to me when I was a child. One night I just prayed to God that they would stop, and they did. That night, I tucked him in and said we should pray. He didn't want to pray with me and said he would do it later when he was alone. I prayed anyway, so he could hear me. I asked him the next day if he prayed about it, and he said he had. The nightmares have stopped.

Dale Faber, a father of three daughters, says using stories from his past gives his girls the permission to be different from their siblings. One episode from the life of his daughter Leah is a good example:

> Leah was four and couldn't wait to go to school like her older sister, Lexie. On those days when we walked Lexie to school, Leah and I watched as she crossed the monkey bars. "When you're ready for school," Lexie told Leah, "you'll be able to do this too." The monkey bars became a symbol of maturity to Leah, who practiced on them faithfully every chance she got. When she was able to cross three bars, her confidence soared.
>
> One day little sister Jessie accompanied us to the school playground. "Watch this, Jessie," Leah said, and she proceeded to cross her three bars before falling. Jessie wanted a try too, and so I lifted her to the bars. She crossed every single rung on

> her first try. Her little sister's success devastated Leah. Her soul was deeply wounded, her self-worth shattered, and I doubted she would recover quickly without some help.
>
> I took her aside and explained that I, too, had been outclassed in physical pursuits when I was younger. "Do you remember Dr. Ron?" I asked her. She nodded to show she remembered our close family friend. "When we were young, he beat me in every sport. He was taller, faster, and stronger. But I realized it didn't matter; I just had to do the best I could, and I also found other things, like schoolwork, that I was really good at."
>
> The little story seemed to cheer her up, but I didn't know it had healed her wounds until the next monkey bar crossing. Jessie was teasing Leah that she could cross the bars and Leah couldn't. Leah said, "So what. Daddy says it doesn't matter. Dr. Ron beat him when they were kids, but Daddy did fine in school." She eventually worked her way across the monkey bars, as I know she'll work her way through life. That's her specialty.

Share and Share Alike

Not all the benefits of being vulnerable and talking about emotions are for the kids. Parents gain a great deal too. Beth Weeden tells about a teachable moment when her only child responded to her with empathy:

> Matt was not one to display affection. He never said, "I love you" or gave compliments and hugs. By the time he was 13 years old, he knew it was a sore spot with me because I had talked about how I needed and wanted affection. One day I hung up from talking to my father, who also tends to be unaf-

> fectionate, but on this day, Dad was the first to say, "I love you." Matt saw how moved I was, and it started a trend. Matt now freely tells both his dad and me that he loves us.

When kids learn how to be empathetic, you can call on those emotions to create a teachable moment. I (Marianne) had no luck trying to get Danielle to be more compassionate through Bible study. Modeling it didn't have much success, either. Because she is so self-confident, she expects everyone around her to act with the same competence, self-assuredness, and bravado. As a result, she's a little unsympathetic to her younger brothers' immaturity as well as to those friends who are reticent or shy. When I said during a teachable moment that I had been one of those unconfident, muddling people when I was in junior high, it got her attention. I was able to put into words the fear and uncertainty shy people face every day. Through my story she was able to understand that some people are afraid of failure, ridicule, or are frightened to try new things. While Danielle probably won't grow up to be a nurse or a psychologist, she can now empathize with people who are not thirsty for adventure or prone to sudden outbursts of high-profile activity.

They Long to Hear the Story

Whether your story is one of God's steady faithfulness since you accepted Christ as a young child or a more recent saga of crisis and conversion, your child needs to know how faith has worked in your life.

Or how it hasn't worked.

Russell grew up as the son of a pioneer missionary in China. Russell's father was a godly man, but he wasn't given to talking much about his own spiritual struggles. As a result, Russell had a hard time relating to his dad. Even today, as a middle-aged man, Russell wishes he'd gotten a chance to know the human side of his father—a legend to whom he feels he'll never measure up.

Your teen needs to see the reality of God in your life, including how your relationship with Him has its ups and downs. It's okay, even beneficial, for your young person to know that you have questions and for the two of you to go to the Bible together for answers.

A great parent-teen session is for each of you to take turns tracing your spiritual pilgrimage on a sheet of paper in a game called "Mountaintops and Valleys." As you draw a mountaintop, representing a high point in your walk with Christ, or a valley, which represents a low point, you give a brief description of what happened and what you learned from it.

Telling your spiritual story isn't just a onetime event, either. Your teen needs to see how you walk with God daily. For example, do you try to have a quiet time? How does it work? What about it frustrates you? How do you pray about difficult things? What if God doesn't seem to answer? Do you ever get mad at God? Does He ever seem distant?

When your teen sees that your experience with God includes doubts, euphoria, emptiness, fullness, satisfaction, grumpiness, failing, and forgiveness, he or she will be more likely to understand that your experience has relevance. It's tough to have a relationship with a legend, but all-too-human believers can make great parents—and spiritual mentors.

Vulnerability and Relationship

Vulnerability is one key to intimacy in a relationship. It takes the parent and child to a deeper level of understanding and appreciation of the other. If your child never learns of your physical, emotional, social, and spiritual struggles, you may be setting up a false image, one they can't measure up to or relate to.

Kids need to hear the successes and failures in your life; your doubts, your triumphs, your times of loneliness, your times of euphoria, your times of disappointment with God, your times of answered prayer, your times of blessing, and your times of waiting. Then they are more likely to understand how you can relate to them and their situations.

When I (Jim) was in flight school, I took my first-stage flight. I started up the engines. My first solo flight in a jet. At first it was okay; I was flying around, doing touch-and-go landings, but I couldn't hear the tower because the weather information was bleeding through the navigational radio. So I turned the navigational radio off to hear the tower. When I requested a pattern change, the only thing I could hear was my own shortened breath and the engines. Suddenly, another plane joined my pattern. I never heard him call an entry. When I came to the overhead pattern, there was another plane. I didn't hear that one call to enter either. I got on the radio and identified myself, but I couldn't get any response. I decided to land. As I started the descent, I put down the flaps and speed brake. When I came across the threshold, I saw two flares. They meant "go around again," but no one had ever told me that. When I came down to land, I forgot to put down the landing gear. The plane hitting the runway was like the sound of

Things I Wish My Parents Had Done Differently

- "Emphasized personal devotions more."
- "Had more home spiritual development, such as family devotions, family nights, and one-on-one talks."
- "Made spiritual training more of an everyday thing, rather than a huge lump every few months."
- "Shared personal stories of spiritual conflict within their lives."
- "I wish that my parents would have just asked us openly what we thought about what was happening around us so that they could explain how God was working."

ten thousand fingernails scratching a chalkboard. *I'm gonna blow up.* There are sparks all over and a full tank of gas.

I didn't blow up, but I sure had messed up. I could not blame anyone else for the damage to a T-37 jet trainer and the danger I had created for the other pilots and myself; I had no out, no excuse. Later, I found out that when I had turned off one radio, the other went off as well.

Feet of Clay

When you blow it in front of your child, these five steps can help restore and improve your relationship in the long run through a teachable moment.

1. All parents make mistakes, choose poorly, get tired and cranky, act selfishly—in short, all parents sin. And one painful day your child will realize it. It's only a matter of time before the hero image becomes tarnished, or worse, topples completely through something traumatic like a divorce, extramarital affair, or physically violent outburst. You must acknowledge your sin.

2. When sin happens in front of or against your child, parents must use those times to apologize and ask their child's forgiveness. By explaining about and asking for forgiveness, you create a teachable moment to explain about God's forgiveness through Jesus Christ.

3. When the gospel of forgiveness is shared, Jesus is revealed as the true hero. Only when the parent-hero image is given up can a perfect Hero take its place.

4. If you don't replace the lost parent-hero image with Christ's image, you leave your child with no one to look up to, no hero.

5. As a result of the apology, your relationship with your child is closer and stronger because it is held together with Jesus' perfection, not yours. And you present a new model to follow, one of humility. Now your children can see how to ask for forgiveness too.

—mkh

But it wasn't the end of the episode. It was the beginning. I had to start all over and get back in a cockpit to fly again.

I have used that story to tell my kids that you can't give up, especially with things of God. Even when we crash our airplanes, we have to get back in and try to soar, letting Him be the wind beneath our wings.

Vulnerability is not a weakness; it is part of the human experience. By being open and honest with them, our children will be open and honest with us. They need to know we have problems too. Through those bad times, we have the privilege of creating teachable moments that show our kids how to rely on the Lord and His strength.

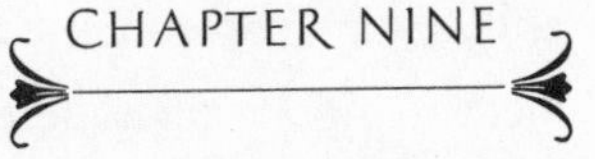

CHAPTER NINE

Milestone Moments

There's a Web site called *Where's George?* for people who have way too much time on their hands. Once you log in, you can enter the serial number of a dollar bill and track the cities it has been in. The site also allows you to guess where the bill will show up in the future by studying the pattern of other dollar bills. *Where's George?* fulfills a natural human interest to know where something has been and anticipate where it will go next.

In the same way, children long to know where they've been. There's no four-year-old who can look at his or her baby pictures without feeling a sense of pride and accomplishment. He has learned to walk, talk, dress without assistance, run, sing, draw, and say the ABC's. As soon as toddlers can talk, they express a desire to be big, to experience new things. They want to know what they are going to do next. Kindergarten children want to tie their shoes; third graders want to master the multiplication tables. Elementary school kids want to move to middle school. Middle school preteens dream about high school. And so it goes; all children long to reach the next mark on the maturity map. It's part of the human condition.

At the Weidmanns' house, Jim and Janet mark the height of each child every year on a special door. If, in one of the growth years, they were to notice no difference in a child's height, they would panic. They'd want to take that child to the Mayo Clinic right away! Milestone moments satisfy a natural hunger people have to anticipate and celebrate spiritual growth—to chart faith development. Milestones allow parents to gauge the spiritual growth of their children; if there is no growth or it's slow, then parents know to intervene.

Spiritual milestones are not a new concept. For generations the Jewish community has honored a coming-of-age celebration for 13-year-olds now called the *bat mitzvah* (for girls) or *bar mitzvah* (for boys). Even Jesus sought out baptism, and that event marked the beginning of His public ministry. If you use milestone moments as spiritual maturity markers for your children, they will know where they've been and where they are going on their spiritual journey.

Milestones are the most formal teachable moment in that they usually have some sort of ceremony and a structured biblical agenda.

Go the Extra Milestone

Celebrating spiritual milestones is the ultimate teachable moment. Milestones cement the spiritual bond between parent and child, strengthening the relationship so that future teachable moments will have greater impact. The milestone message also marks a profound spiritual truth that signals maturity. Here are eight more reasons to go the extra milestone in your child's spiritual training.

1. Eighty-five percent of people who accept Christ do so between the ages of four and 18. Milestone moments create learning catalysts during the time your child is most naturally receptive to receiving them. The celebrations help you make sure you're at the right place at the right time to teach your child about God.

2. Milestones allow you to set a positive tone of how you will communicate and relate faith concepts to your child. Your children will

know they can talk to you about deep spiritual matters and receive a loving response.

3. When parents commit to using milestones, it establishes them as the spiritual leaders of the home.

4. Milestone moments produce a blueprint for a spiritual heritage, which can last for generations. When placed side by side, the milestones create a foundation on which your children's spiritual maturity is built.

5. Milestone ceremonies inspire a reverence, hunger, and respect for spiritual growth. Like a girl who longs for her ears to be pierced, her first date, or her driver's license, so your child will look forward to and anticipate the next milestone moment.

6. Milestone moments give parents a platform to address developmental and spiritual issues before they can become problems. The classic example is the milestone Preparing for Adolescence (discussed later). Both of Jim Weidmann's sons stopped him in the middle of their anatomy discussions and said, "Oh, Dad, I'm so glad you told me. I thought I was dying of cancer!" He also told them that their peers were going to judge them on their looks, their intelligence, their money, or their athletic ability. Jim was able to explain that God looks at the heart and that their true identity comes from Him. He encouraged his sons not to let other criteria become an issue.

7. Milestones provide a way for parents to stay involved in their children's spiritual growth. Tracking the milestones provides a calendar of events so that preteen and teen spiritual development is not forgotten or overlooked.

8. Children who experience milestones are equipped with the map that shows how to get to their ultimate destination—eternal life through Jesus Christ.

There are seven milestones, but the five we will mention in this chapter are Baptism, Communion, Preparing for Adolescence, Sexual Purity, and the Rite of Passage (Crossing into Adulthood).

Milestone Moments Are Sealed Through Ceremony

When planning a milestone, keep the tone celebratory. This is similar to a birthday party or high school graduation. New clothes—yes! A special gift—yes! A party—yes!

Next comes planning the actual event. David and Peggy Wilber helped their 10-year-old son plan his baptism. Instead of being baptized at their home church, Michael decided he wanted to be baptized in a lake at a family camp they attended annually. The pastor who baptized him was an uncle; everyone at the campground knew the Wilbers well, and several special, surprise guests arrived to witness the moment. Because Michael helped with the planning, the people who were the most spiritually significant to him could be there—Grandma, cousins, uncles, and aunts. Now a special holiday retreat will also be the place of a milestone memory for Michael.

Just as you would for a birthday party, invite grandparents, other relatives, and any other interested people to milestone moments. These could be your child's Christian classmates, his or her coaches, music teachers, or former teachers. Do whatever it takes to create a charged atmosphere, a sense of grandeur about the occasion. By celebrating baptism as a "Rebirth-in-Christ Day," you have a milestone as a point of reference to say, "Yes, you believe!"

You don't have to do all the planning for a baptism yourself. Your home church will have the structure in place; you can then make sure your child's personal preferences are taken into consideration. You can walk through the ceremony beforehand, giving your child a chance to ask questions and make suggestions. When the day rolls around, the advance planning will ensure your child has every chance to grasp and appreciate the profound spiritual element of baptism.

Author, father, and pastor Robert Lewis, in his book *Raising a Modern-Day Knight,* praises the value of ceremony:

Ceremonies are those special occasions that weave the fabric of human existence. Weddings. Award banquets. Graduations. The day you became an Eagle Scout or were accepted into a fraternity [or sorority]. We remember because of ceremony.

Think back upon the significant moments in your life. With few exceptions, the value of those moments was sealed by a ceremony. Someone took the time to plan the details, prepare the speech, and purchase the awards—so you would feel special.

Ceremony should be one of the crown jewels for helping a boy become a man [or a girl become a woman]....

Ceremonies come in all shapes and sizes. But the truth is, good ceremonies share four common characteristics.

First, memorable ceremonies are costly. The more time, thought, planning, effort, and money you give to a celebration, the more memorable it will be.

For example, you can celebrate your wedding anniversary by giving your wife a nice card with your signature.... But as every woman knows—and every man has discovered, usually the hard way—the best approach is even costlier, such as a card, roses, dinner, and poem you took hours to write. In the language of ceremony, this constitutes a four-bagger, a grand slam. Memorability grows in proportion to cost. The more you give, the greater the impact.

Second, memorable ceremonies ascribe value. By setting aside time, making the effort, spending money, and employing meaningful ceremony, we declare the high value of an individual. At the same time, ceremonies ascribe value to the beliefs and morals we hold important....

Third, memorable ceremonies employ symbols. Weddings are symbolized by a ring, Christmas by a star, graduation by a diploma. Each of these symbols calls to mind a host of pleasant memories....

> Finally, and perhaps most important, memorable ceremonies empower a life with vision.... Ceremony marks the transition from one season to another. It says powerfully, forcefully, and regally, "From this point forward, life is going to be different!"

The goal of milestone celebrations is to put the memory of spiritual growth on your child's map of life.

Here are two more ideas for teachable moment ceremonies:

1. A blessing ceremony. This could range from the very simple (a few people praying over your teen) to the sophisticated (a meal, a formal blessing, prayers, gifts). Before Ed and Christy Smith's son, Eric,

Teen Quotes

From sons:

"Dad, I want you to remind me at least once a month about purity."

"I want my dad to teach me about girls and dating."

"Dad, I wish you would talk to me about sex and spend more time with me."

"I would like my mom to show me things that girls will like when I date them."

From daughters:

"Dad, I wish we would have built a stronger spiritual relationship earlier so it would be easier to talk to you now."

"Dad, I wish you would ask me more about my relationships and keep pushing it in my head not to have sex."

"Mom, I wish you would be more comfortable when we discuss things because that would make me more comfortable."

"Mom, I wish you would have talked to me when I was young. Now that you've waited until I'm older, I feel uncomfortable since it's unusual."

—compiled by Karie Hughes and Passion and Principles

left for college out of state, they wanted to send him off with a blessing. They invited his closest friends and their parents, as well as family and church members. All gathered at the Smiths' house for refreshments and conversation, and then the spotlight was focused on Eric. Many of the people talked about qualities in Eric they admired and ways they had seen him grow over the years. Others offered encouragement and advice for thriving in college. The ceremony ended with several people praying a special blessing on his life in the years ahead. For Eric—and everyone involved—it was a deeply meaningful and moving time.

2. A Christian *bar mitzvah* (*bat mitzvah* for girls). If you've been to a traditional *bar mitzvah* or *bat mitzvah*, you know how sacred and inspiring these ceremonies are. A *bar mitzvah* takes place when a Jewish boy reaches his 13th birthday and attains the age of religious duty and responsibility. The idea here is to weave Christian themes into the Jewish model, which usually involves reciting revered Bible passages, taking an oath or verbal commitment to the faith, commemorating the step from child to adult, and then feasting and partying.

Milestones Reinforce Spiritual Truths

The first time little Josh saw a communion celebration, he was brokenhearted that he didn't get to participate. He told his mother, "Everybody else got a snack, and I didn't get anything!"

Most children want to take part in this rite of passage, but many can't understand its significance until they are older, about eight or nine. With this milestone, your child enters into the rite of Christian remembrance, memorializing the birth, death, resurrection, and return of Jesus Christ.

If explained correctly through a teachable moment, you can be sure your kids understand the symbolism and spiritual benefits the ceremony offers. If you look down the church pew the Weidmanns sit in, you'll see four children with bowed heads. Because they take Communion seriously, they look upon the bread and the cup with reverence.

Communion also represents Christ's salvation message. By the time Sean Bruner was nine years old, he understood the salvation symbolism in the ceremony because his parents had impressed the significance of it into his heart. One Sunday, his Uncle Joe, a non-Christian, came to a church service with the Bruners. During the preparatory message of Communion, the gospel was presented. At the opening of the ceremony, Sean asked Uncle Joe, "What about you, Uncle Joe? Have you accepted Jesus?"

He answered, "We'll talk about it later."

When the plate came around to Joe, Sean said, "Well, have you or haven't you?" He was worried that Joe would take Communion without first preparing his heart.

For Sean's father, Kurt, the moment held a little tension, but he couldn't help but be pleased his son understood and recognized the significance of Communion.

If parents take the time to ensure their kids know the meaning of this milestone, every Communion can be a teachable moment about Christ's sacrifice on the cross. Not only do milestones help kids remember specific biblical truths but they also help children live them out.

Milestones Help Prepare for the Future

All milestones help kids look to the spiritual road ahead. After a milestone moment, children can study their spiritual journey map and plan for their life. They can anticipate the spiritual valleys and mountains, the meadows and rocky terrain. The Preparing for Adolescence milestone helps kids prepare for their adult future. Jim Weidmann, in the book *Spiritual Milestones,* shares his thoughts about how difficult adolescence can be and why our children need guidance:

I was in my second year at the Air Force Academy, and this would be one of my toughest hurdles so far—surviving a mock prisoner of war camp. The instructor said we'd go through a lot of training in our careers, training that would make the Air Force a much better organization. But this experience was for our benefit, not for the Air Force's. You see, military experts discovered that the greatest, most debilitating fear of any prisoner is the sheer terror of the unknown. So our prisoner training was developed for the sole purpose of exposing us to what possibly could happen.

No, we wouldn't be tortured or starved. But we'd find out about pain, and we'd definitely get hungry. By experiencing (at least in our minds) the worst that could happen—and learning the best ways to cope—we could take comfort in knowing we'd been prepared. If we ever landed in a prison camp, the terror might be muted a bit. We could expect to survive it.

Now I don't mean to equate entering adolescence to walking through the gates of a dark and dingy prison camp in some God-forsaken jungle! But let's face it: growing up can be pretty scary. Do you remember it—your first pimple? First period? First date? And even more devastating—your initial realization that the wonderful world of adult freedom comes packaged with serious doses of responsibility and accountability?

Standing on the cutting edge of development, hovering between childhood and adulthood, the budding adolescent faces fear and trepidation. And as we observe his forays into the grown-up world, we see a herky-jerky, start-and-stop comedy of errors. Sometimes it's two steps backward (into unbelievably childish behaviors) for every one step forward into mature and wise decision-making.

As parents, we are there for one purpose: to prepare our

Signs and Wonders

Symbols enhance and give a concrete way to commemorate a milestone. Also, adding a new dynamic to your child's spiritual responsibilities helps him or her see that maturity is coming. Here's what we recommend:

MILESTONE	SYMBOL	PRIVILEGE
Baptism	Certificate	Increased participation in family devotions/lead in prayer.
Communion	Communion chalice with his or her name engraved on it	Can reflect more deeply about Communion.
Preparing for Adolescence	Let the child choose something that represents him or her. *Example for girls:* a charm for a bracelet *Example for boys:* a pocket knife	Parents to determine one new responsibility and one new privilege.
Purity	Ring	More trust from parents. For example, be allowed to double date with supervision.
Rite of Passage	Family cross, family crest, a sword (for boys), a heart necklace or charm bracelet (for girls)	Some suggestions: • Lead the family prayer time. • Lead a family night. • Take over an adult role when a parent is absent. • Seek new responsibilities at church.

adolescent for this incredible transformation into a responsible, mature citizen in adult society. So in this "Preparing for Adolescence" Milestone Moment, remember that your child is experiencing so much change that your mentoring time needs to reveal and explain the unknown—covering all the myriad transformations that are about to occur. The intent of this teachable moment is to lessen the terror, to identify the social, emotional, physical, and identity issues in the light of spiritual understanding. This will equip your child with the knowledge of how to grow through all the dramatic changes in a peaceful, godly way.

The Preparing for Adolescence milestone moment works well when it takes place over a weekend. And listening to an audio version of Dr. Dobson's *Preparing for Adolescence* is highly recommended. After experiencing this milestone, parents have treasured memories of the many teachable moments it created. Janet Weidmann recalls her weekend with daughter Janae:

> I'll never forget the weekend Janae and I enjoyed together. We put the date on our calendar weeks in advance, which added to our anticipation of the trip. I told Janae that we were going to be talking about the things that were ahead of her as she moved from girlhood into womanhood. I didn't mention too much about the fact that we'd be dealing with the topic of sexual intimacy, since that is only a portion of the information covered by Dr. James Dobson in his wonderful tape series "Preparing for Adolescence."
>
> Janae and I got into the van after bidding our family goodbye and headed for a town about an hour's drive away. I'd already made the motel reservations and was looking forward to a wonderful weekend with my precious daughter. I had packed

all of the necessities to give her a manicure and pedicure and to be able to braid and play with her hair while we were listening to the tapes and talking. Of course, we also took our swimsuits so we could hit the motel pool.

As we started down the highway, I explained to Janae that I would put in the first tape, but if, at any time, she had a question or comment, she should feel free to stop the tape and we would discuss it. To listen to Dr. Dobson's voice on these tapes was like having an invisible third friend in the car with us. How thankful I was that he was doing the explaining on some of the issues! I know Jim felt the same way when he went off on his milestone moment with our two boys....

Janae and I had an incredibly wonderful and memorable weekend, and we still get a warm, fuzzy feeling as we pass "our motel" when we go through that town. We can recall so many things: the times when we laughed, when we walked hand-in-hand, when we lay in the grass and whispered while looking up at the starry sky, the times when Janae sat in stunned disbelief that her mom and dad would do such things! We created special memories we'll both cherish forever.

When explaining to other parents what we do with our children during this venture into preparing for adolescence, many say, "My child would be so embarrassed!" or "My child will totally clam up and not talk to me about these things." Yet we've found that if we let the line out little by little and set up light discussion topics beforehand, it has made our weekend away much more successful. Let me explain. During the week prior to getting away for this weekend, you might say to your child, "I'm so looking forward to our time away together. I'd really like to understand what you already know about some of the things we'll be dealing with—sex, for instance. What have you learned so far through your friends, television, or elsewhere?" These little "set-ups" can help to make the weekend more comfortable for both of you.

Parents, I know this can be a very uncomfortable weekend for you and your child because of the subject matter. After all, many of us were never presented with these "facts of life" in a biblical context. Therefore, be extra sensitive to your children as you listen to them and try to understand their street knowledge and experience with each of these issues.

Milestones prepare your children for the Christian walk in the following ways: Baptism establishes their inheritance with Christ; Communion cleanses them for a daily relationship with Jesus; preparing for adolescence helps them anticipate and successfully negotiate becoming a teen; and a rite of passage equips them for adulthood.

Milestones Provide a Reference Point

Some subjects are so intense that a single teachable moment or milestone celebration can't do justice to the topic. Sex is one of those intense subjects. My (Jim's) older children attend a church with a great youth group. There, the kids accepted purity rings and went over the reasons to wait for sex until marriage. But I wanted to make sure they understood everything, so I created a teachable moment using the "gift box" example.

I always try to make sure my kids hear important messages several times in different ways. The more creative the process, the more unique the moment, the easier it is for them to remember. So I created a teachable moment to refine the purity concept. I sat them on a couch—Joshua, Jacob, and Janae—and said, "Listen, I have a present for each of you." I handed each of them a beautifully wrapped present. Confusion registered on their faces after the paper had been torn off, because they each held a sibling's favorite candy bar.

I feigned an apology. "Oops, I messed up. I gave you the wrong gifts. Here's some masking tape. See if you can fix the package." Well, they did the best they could and re-wrapped the gifts. Then they swapped the gifts so the favorite candy matched the right person. For the second time, they unwrapped the gifts.

"Well," I asked, "how was it?"

Joshua said, "It wasn't special. We already knew what it was."

"Ah-ha!" I said. "It's just like purity. It's a gift we can truly give only once. You don't want to give it away outside of marriage or it's just not that special—it's not pure."

But even with a solid program at church and a good teachable moment, that lesson is not "all wrapped up." Once you set the groundwork for sexual purity through a milestone moment, you can use general discussions—less formal teachable moments—to reinforce the concept. You need to cover the areas of lust vs. love vs. infatuation. You've got to let your children know that they will feel lust, be infatuated and one day fall in love. Maybe they'll even fall out of love. If this

Talk About Sex

A September 2002 report from the *Journal of Adolescent Health* reveals, "Close relationships with parents, especially the mom, can often delay the start of a teen's sexual activity."

The author of the study, Dr. Robert Blum, director of the University of Minnesota's Center for Adolescent Health and Development, has said: "Teens [girls] who feel closer to their mother, especially young teens, are less likely to start having sex. And children whose parents know their kids' friends and have conversations with their friends' parents also delay becoming sexually active longer."

Among the other findings cited in the report are…

- Mothers can influence their daughters' sexual behavior by clearly communicating their strong disapproval of premarital sex.

is the human condition, if this is the real world, how should they deal with all that?

Your children need to know that people—yes, even Christians—have a tendency to lean toward impurity, and they must learn how to control their thoughts and focus on what's pure and stay away from what's not.

We have follow-up teachable moments, too. Usually, it's while we're picking a movie to watch. I ask, "Should we watch an R-rated movie (usually not) or what about a PG 13-rated movie?" We will go into those discussions about what can take root in our hearts, why we should we guard what we put in, and ask questions like "Would watching this film help us focus on what's pure?" The formal milestone moment sets up the informal teachable moment. It's easier because you've already established the baseline.

Robert Lewis explained to his son about sex and his role as a man during his preparing-for-adolescence milestone:

- The absence of a close relationship between mothers and their older adolescent daughters seems to increase the likelihood of sexual intercourse.
- When adolescents perceive that they have good family relationships, as well as opportunities and parental support for achievement in school, a delay in onset of sexual activity is seen.
- Although mothers tend to underestimate the sexual activity of their adolescents, when they do suspect their child is sexually active or on the verge of becoming sexually active, they are generally correct.

The conclusion of the study? "Parents need to be clear about their values and then clearly articulate them to their children and adolescents."

Wow! Modern science confirms what God told the Israelites to do centuries ago—impress your children with solid values.

Our talks were lively, sometimes explicit (we talked candidly about sex), and relationally bonding for father and son. At the conclusion of our study (which I coordinated with his 13th birthday), I prepared a simple ceremony and took Garrett to dinner and let him order any meal on the menu. He chose his favorite: steak.

For an hour, the two of us sat and talked about adolescence and manhood and his growing responsibilities. At this time, I introduced the manhood definition:… "A man is someone who rejects passivity, accepts responsibility, leads courageously, and expects the greater reward—God's reward." I explained these phrases and illustrated each concept in a simple way.

I then asked Garrett to memorize the definition, which he did almost immediately. I told him this would be the "North Star" for his manhood and that I planned to refer to it often in the years ahead. We then finished this special ceremonial occasion with my prayer for God's blessing in his life.

The unexpected surprises arising from that ceremony came later. Since that time, I've been amazed at how many opportunities I've had to shape my son's behavior by referring to our definition of manhood. This is the beauty of clarifying and defining values.

I remember the time our family went out to dinner and Garrett charged into the restaurant, forgetting to hold the door for his mother and sisters. I stopped him in mid-stride and said, "Hey, what does a real man do in a situation like this?"

Garrett immediately said, "Well, Dad, I guess a real man accepts responsibility for the women he's with." Bingo.

"So, instead of charging into the restaurant," I replied, "act the gentleman and become a door holder."

Once you've defined manhood for your son, small day-to-day experiences such as this become opportunities to reinforce a biblical portrait of manhood.

My wife, Sherard, told me a few months ago about a girl at school who took an interest in Garrett. Another young lady, acting as a mediator for this budding relationship, began calling him on the phone to explore the possibility of romance with her friend.

Garrett pondered this for a while. Then one night he took charge and called the interested girl directly. He told her he couldn't be her boyfriend.

Sherard overheard the conversation (no, she wasn't listening on the extension), and when Garrett hung up, she complimented him on the way he had handled the situation. Without hesitation, almost matter-of-factly, Garrett replied, "Mom, a real man must reject passivity and accept responsibility for things like this!"

Nothing warms a father's heart like progress.

Even our daughters, Elizabeth and Rebekah—both older than Garrett—have benefited from our ongoing discussion. They have heard us refer again and again to the characteristics of an authentic man. Whether they realize it or not, they are subconsciously forming an image of what real men are like.

Because sex and adulthood are such pervasive and broad topics, they need to be handled in creative ways throughout your child's teen years. Establishing a preparing-for-adolescence, rite-of-passage, and a sexual-purity milestone gives parents points of reference on the map to discuss those issues through follow-up teachable moments during their teens' formative years.

Milestones Show Your Children Where They're Going

A milestone moment prepares your child for the future by providing necessary knowledge. Milestones also help shape a vision for the joy of the Christian life. Baptism points to salvation; Communion points to life with Christ and in Christ; preparing for adolescence takes the mystery out of puberty; sexual purity points toward a holy marriage and the gift of sacrifice; and the rite of passage points toward a future of service to the Lord.

A Right—On Rite of Passage

When Allan Mesko drove his son, Brian, to the Ozark Conference Center about an hour west of Little Rock, the 16-year-old thought he and his dad were simply going to spend the night on the mountain. But Allan had other plans.

They checked in with the couple who managed the camp, and soon this couple's son invited Brian to go for a walk. As the two teenagers strolled down a path, suddenly the headmaster at Brian's Christian school stepped out from behind a tree. Brian's first thought was He must be staying at the lodge.

But after a quick greeting, the other boy returned home. Brian and his headmaster continued walking, the older man explaining that Brian's father had asked him to share some thoughts on the subject of manhood. Bible in hand, he turned to the books of 1 and 2 Timothy and highlighted specific passages relevant to manhood.

After a while, the two came to a teepee, and Brian saw a friend inside. This man took the headmaster's place. Walking past ponds and through open meadows, he talked with Brian about different choices he would face as a man. He also made a statement Brian will never forget: "Brian, maybe one day you'll be making this walk with my son."

The pair headed into the woods, where a teacher at Brian's school was

A few weeks before my (Jim's) son Jacob's rite-of-passage milestone, I had a teachable moment about his pastoral gifts. It was just after he told me four Mormons had called him into a discussion about the deity of Christ.

"Let me get this straight," I said. "Today you told four Mormon kids that Jesus is the Creator, and they were dumbfounded?"

"Yeah," he said. "I guess that's what happened."

"That was an incredible thing to do," I said. "Did you enjoy it?"

"You know, I really did."

seated on a bench. His part was to cover the characteristics of manhood. After a while, the two headed back to the lodge, with Brian assuming that the surprises were now over. They weren't. Four other adult friends were at the lodge waiting for him. Allan grilled some expensive steaks, and the celebrants drank soft drinks out of Mason jars. After dinner, the group gathered in a circle, and each man noted special qualities he had seen in Brian. The young man was speechless.

Allan then presented his son with James Dobson's book *Life on the Edge,* signed by all the men. He also gave his son a plaque, which read: "To my son, Brian Benjamin Mesko, in recognition of your initiation into the community of men. With much love and joy, Dad." To conclude the ceremony, the men gathered around Brian and prayed for him.

Before they left the camp the next morning, Allan and Brian walked the same course Brian had traveled the evening before. The young man repeated what he'd heard and pointed out to his father the key locations. Later, while Brian was occupied with the camp manager's son, Allan drove the same course in his car to take pictures. He later presented the photographs to Brian.

"When I think about that night, I am overwhelmed with joy," Brian says. "I'm so grateful for a dad who would do something like that."

"What you told them was right on doctrinally—you're good at that," I said. "That's one of your strengths! And you like it! This is what it means to be gifted in that area."

It's important for teens to know that God has equipped them to serve in ways that bring fulfillment. There is no greater joy in life than discovering the gifts God has given you and applying them. Through a rite-of-passage milestone, you can help your child discover and affirm those gifts. This can be done informally through spontaneous teachable moments or formally through a rite of passage. I recommend using both.

A rite of passage is basically a time of fellowship with mentors selected by the child. Around age 15, kids shut down and are less receptive to teaching. So I really wanted to solidify the concept in my children's minds that they have a solid destiny and validity in Christ. I went over the top in my preparation, but I can't overemphasize how important this milestone moment is.

I'll describe a little of what we did for Jacob. I said to him, "I want you to identify six men who have made a spiritual impact on your life." Over the weeks, we met for breakfast with the chosen men and talked about different aspects of the Christian life. The mentor shared how God had worked in his life. For the final ceremony, each man came with three questions for Jacob, and he got to ask them questions as well.

The topics of discussion were adulthood and how to handle the different aspects of becoming a man or woman of God. (See chapter 11 for discussion topics for the rite of passage.) Because we'd been affirming Jacob's spiritual gifts for a few years, at the age of 14 he had discovered those gifts and was looking for a place to use them. During one part of Jacob's rite of passage, he had the opportunity to share with his mentors why he felt he was ready to be a spiritual man. He told them about an incident that had taken place the week before:

> I was at a Revival Generation meeting of about five thousand people in South Carolina, and my brother, Joshua, was in

charge. About 20 minutes before it started, he said, "Hey, Jake, I need you to make a speech." Then he said, "We need something peppy, something fun." So I used the example of my walk with Christ being like Dorothy's walk on the yellow brick road. I knew there were some things I needed in this relationship; the first thing I needed was the mind of Christ. How would I know what Jesus would do if I didn't have the mind of Christ? So I did the impression of the scarecrow and I sang the little song. By this time, the crowd was going nuts.

I talked about the next character that Dorothy ran into, the tin man. He needed a heart. And I told them that I needed a heart of passion for God. I did the impression of the tin man, and then I went on to the lion. I said I found out that I needed the courage to stand up for my faith.

The speech went over well, and everyone was laughing, but I didn't think it had that great of an impact, that is until this big guy motioned me over to the front of the stage. He said, "There's this girl down here, and she needs to talk to you." So I looked down at this 13-year-old girl, and I could tell she'd been crying because there was mascara running down her face. She held up this beat-up little teddy bear. I took it, and I could see from the look in her eyes that it meant so much to her. She wanted a hug, and so I lay down on the stage, reached over the edge, and with one arm gave her a hug. I told her, "I'll come find you afterward because I want to talk to you."

After the event, I ran off the stage, pushed through the crowd, and found her. She broke out crying again. Holding up the bear, I said, "Why did you give me this?"

She said, "When you were up there on stage, you gave me hope. Ever since the shootings at Columbine, I didn't know what hope was. I didn't know where to find it."

Then I walked around to the back of the stage, and the big guy said, "What did she say to you?"

I said, "She's really nice and everything...."

There was a pause, and he said, "There are a couple of things you need to know about that girl. Number one, that teddy bear is her comfort; that is her all. She's had it since she was born; that's everything she has. The second thing you need to realize is that girl is deaf, and I signed your speech to her. She came to Christ."

It was at that point I realized that through me God can make the deaf hear. It was God's affirmation that I'm a spiritual man and I need to take on the responsibilities of a spiritual man.

Milestones Are a Time to Affirm

Spiritual milestones convey to your child that you love him enough to create a special time to teach him. The time and expense involved, both monetarily and emotionally, are worth it. They will leave your children with memories—milestone markers—to cherish and cling to when they leave home and must choose which path to follow.

Conveying your blessing to your children can be done with fanfare. Children need and long to hear that they are growing up in a way that pleases both you and God. Here's a letter that Janet Weidmann wrote to Jacob for his rite of passage:

Jacob,

From the moment they placed you in my arms, I knew you were a gift from God. In those precious moments following your birth, I thought about how wonderful it would be for you and your big brother to become best buddies, and it's been so much fun to see your relationship unfold. You have always held such a special place within our family. A joy and a gentleness surround you.

You were a cuddler as a little boy, always coming downstairs in your cute football pajamas and crawling up on my lap for a morning snuggle. You no longer climb on my lap—thank goodness!—but you're always there to give me a hug when you walk by, telling me how much you love me. You're such an encourager when I need a little lift.

Jacob, you are now not only my son, you are one of my best friends. Raising you has been a joyous journey, and I look forward with anticipation to the years ahead.

Today, I bless you with a mother's heart that is full of enormous pride in the child you were, the young man that you are, and the incredibly awesome man you will become. I have prayed many things for you, even from the time you were in my womb, and I bless into your life those things I have prayed for you. I bless you with an honest heart, filled with the utmost integrity; a tender and compassionate spirit; a strong and healthy body; many deep and loyal friendships; a loving and devoted wife and children; courage and strength of character to face all of the challenges life will bring; days full of joy.

Most of all, I pray that you will always enjoy a deep relationship with God all the days of your life.

You will always have my love and my blessing, Jacob. I am so proud to be the one you call "Mom."

I love you so,

Mom

The overriding purpose of milestone moments is to affirm that your child is on the right road, heading toward a life with God. After Jesus' baptism His Father said, "This is my son, whom I love; with him I am well pleased" (Matthew 3:17). In a like manner we need to let our kids know they are pleasing to us—and to God.

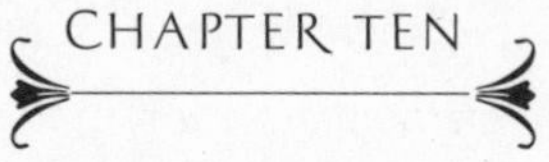

CHAPTER TEN

Parents' Questions Answered

Q: How do I strike a balance between seizing every possible teaching moment and overdoing it?

A: Timing is everything. Use your relationship radar to tell if the moment is right. If you're still unsure, err on the side of silence. You don't want to spoil a good family fun time with a lesson that won't be appreciated. You can let an occasional object lesson pass, but if your child is the one who is the catalyst, move! When that question pops up or he or she does something that begs for a conversation, don't miss that opportunity. Work on removing any rhinestones from your teaching repertoire, and the diamonds will sparkle even brighter.

Q: What if my son rolls his eyes while I'm talking about God?

A: Stop talking and discipline him in a firm, fair, and calm manner. For example, send him to his room until dinner with no use of electronic devices.

His disrespectful behavior is a clue that your relationship needs work; no child will respect an adult (or a teachable moment) if he or she is allowed to be uncivil. After the discipline is over, make a date with your son for an activity of his choice, and have fun. After a few days of good behavior on his part, and when he can receive advice from you on other subjects such as sports, homework, or friendships, then you are ready to try another spiritual teachable moment. For a while, focus only on building up your parent-son relationship so that instead of rolling his eyes at you, he can say, "Hey, Dad, I don't agree with what you said, and here's why...." And begin to ask him questions; putting part of the conversation responsibility in his lap will lessen the chance he'll respond with criticism or more rolling eyes.

Q: What do I do if the teachable moment didn't sink in?

A: Dr. James Dobson uses the example of the cocklebur to encourage parents that one day their teachable moments will yield results:

> Have you ever had the experience of walking through an open field in late summer and feeling the sting of small cockleburs in your shoes and around your ankles? Those thin, brown weeds are armed with dozens of sharp spines that grab our socks and eventually work their way into the skin. They're terribly annoying.
>
> But let me tell you something interesting about cockleburs. Inside those prickly seed pods are not just one, but several seeds, and they germinate in different years. If the first seed fails to sprout one year, due to a drought or other poor conditions, the second is still waiting in the ground. When the next season rolls around, it begins to open and grow. But if that one doesn't take root, there is still a third seed waiting for the year after that. They are the original "time release" capsules. I was thinking the other day about these cockleburs as they relate to children. We parents work so hard to teach certain concepts and civilities to our kids in the hopes that some of them are going to take root and grow. But many of those seeds fail to

germinate, and the effort seems in vain. The good news, however, is that this instruction can also be like a time-release capsule. It may lie dormant for a decade or more and then suddenly break through the ground and sprout.

The key is to remain faithful to the cause—to continue planting seeds and not to get discouraged. The harvest may be in years to come, but it's worth the wait.

Q: Can I use teachable moments with my toddlers?

A: Absolutely—if you concentrate on teaching simple concepts about God's love and creation and tell some easy-to-understand Bible stories. You can also affirm your child's good behavior through a teachable moment. Keep in mind, however, that you won't see much changed behavior until your child can understand the concepts of delayed gratification and consequences, as well as express his or her wishes clearly. That development normally comes somewhere around age four.

Your main rule of thumb for young children is this: When they are grown, they should be able to say, "I can't remember a day in my life when I didn't know that God and my parents loved me."

Q: Do teachable moments work for grandchildren?

A: If grandparents have a good relationship with their grandchildren—yes! Teachable moments work well within the context of any secure adult-child relationship.

Q: My daughter is a junior in college. How can I adapt the teachable-moment concept for adult children?

A: You can be a mentor to your daughter, even when you are 107 and she is a spry 80. The key is in allowing your daughter to change from a dependent teen/college student into an independent adult child, and then to a wife and mother.

There are milestones for the adult years, such as her wedding, that you'll want to commemorate and help her through. The truths that you will want to discuss with her will change as she does, and you probably should steer clear of object lessons or anything else that could sound patronizing. Keep your relationship healthy, and she'll still want and need your advice. If you wait for her to ask a question, then you can still share from your experience and point her in the direction of the Scriptures.

Q: Should I try a teachable moment if my children's friends are there?

A: It's very rare for a teachable moment to work with friends around. The timing is usually poor, because your child is focused on his or her friends and not you. Plus, it may embarrass your child.

In some families, however, there are friends who are so comfortable and at ease in your home that they are practically family. If that is the case, here are three guidelines to consider before using a teachable moment when your child's friend is present: (1) How good is your relationship with the visitor? Would he or she be comfortable praying with you? If you have a good spiritual relationship, the teaching will have a good chance to take root. (2) Will this teachable moment draw your child and the friend closer, or will it create tension instead? (3) What is the nature of the teachable moment? Is it appropriate to have someone else listening? Your child might be embarrassed receiving a compliment or talking about sexual-purity issues.

Q: What if I know there's a verse in the Bible that refers to the teachable moment but I can't remember it exactly?

A: You can't wait to teach your children about God until you have the entire Bible memorized. Paraphrase the verse as best you can and either look it up as soon as you can or challenge older children to find it. If you make a game out of it, you can use the memory lapse as a way to extend the teaching moment.

Q: Object lessons sound like extended analogies or metaphors. I hated that in school. Do you have any advice for me?

A: Stick with what you know. If the list of object lessons in chapter 11 reminds you of freshman English class, don't use them. Instead, focus on using teachable moments to teach concrete faith principles and to develop an awareness of God's love.

Q: My children know more about the Bible than I do. Should I still try a teachable moment?

A: Yes. You can use their knowledge instead of being intimidated by it. Ask them questions like "What do you know about the fall of Jericho?" or "What does the Bible say about giving to the poor?" Let them know you're interested in learning too. That way, you're modeling humility and a willingness to increase your knowledge.

Q: My children need to learn everything. Where should I start?

A: Let the catalysts be your guide. Always try, however, to stick to a basic truth about a fundamental Christian concept. Almost any teachable moment can be wrapped up with one of the following ideas: (1) God loves us; that's why we're to follow that principle. (2) That's why we need Jesus to forgive our sins and redeem us. (3) That's one of the ways God shows us He loves us. (4) Christians aren't of this world; we have a spiritual guide, the Holy Spirit, and so we do things differently.

Q: I'm sure my kids won't listen to a teachable moment because they can smell a lecture a hundred miles away. What should I do?

A: All kids can love learning, because knowledge increases their personal power and sense of self-worth. And whether they admit it or not, learning is intellectually stimulating. Spiritual knowledge will satisfy your children's souls, because all humans are pre-wired to wonder about God. That mix makes teaching and learning about God natural.

If they're lecture-shy, it may be for a valid reason. Ask them to tell you what they think a lecture is and take mental notes. Then follow up with "Okay, if I want to teach you something, what's the best way to do it?" Listen, and when practical, apply their suggestions. Asking them questions takes away the lecture feel and helps keep the discussion focused on what's important to them.

Q: Is it wrong to sometimes just have fun with my children without looking to turn situations into teachable moments?

A: By all means have fun; the more the better. The merriment you have with your kids will make teachable moments more effective in the long run. Whoop it up!

Q: By the time I get home from work, I'm exhausted and ready to veg out. I don't have the energy to think. How am I supposed to relate to my kids when I'm so tired?

A: Cheer up and take some time in the evenings for yourself. Teachable moments can occur at any time, any place; they don't have to be after work. In fact, if your heart is not in the task, your kids will know it. Teachable moments take very little physical effort, but you do have to be mentally in tune and available for your children. Instead, plan ahead for teachable moments during your scheduled date time with your children, or have some questions ready for those short trips in the car.

Q. What about a teachable-moment movie night?

A: See page 122 for an example.

Q: I'm not a natural teacher. Are you sure I can do this?

A: Yes! What makes you the perfect teacher for your child is that you are his or her parent. That special bond far outweighs any experience or personality trait "natural" teachers may have. If your relationship with your child is healthy, then that relationship is what gives you an automatic teaching credential; your child will listen because there is love between you. God will equip you! Pray along with the author of Hebrews who wrote, "May the God of peace…equip you with everything good for doing his will" (Hebrews 13:20-21).

Q: My child goes to Sunday school and youth group. Isn't that enough?

A: Sunday school and youth group are a good foundation for Bible study. But because the learning occurs in such a large group, it's difficult to find out if your child has internalized or absorbed the lessons. An old saying goes, "The longest distance in the world is the space between the head and the heart." Unless we interact with our children and ask them faith questions, we won't know if they are applying or even believing the lessons taught at church. A good way to plan a teachable moment is to find out what is being taught in Sunday school and other church classes. That way you can reinforce those concepts with teachable moments later.

CHAPTER ELEVEN

101 Common Opportunities for Uncommon Teaching

Think of your best teachable moments as 60-second commercials for God's truth and leave the 30-minute infomercial "lectures" where they belong—on late-night cable TV. The scenarios and Bible verses provided are for you to pick and choose from. Should a completely different idea materialize—go with it. At a later time you may want to use the extra truths and verses as a base for a family Bible study, but don't ruin the beauty of the teachable moment by cramming too many verses into one sound bite.

Remember these rules for a positive teachable moment:

- Use questions to start the conversation and keep it going.
- Give your child the opportunity to explain the spiritual truth if he or she can.
- Affirm every respectful attempt at an answer.
- Keep it light.
- Stay focused on the catalyst.
- Explain truths in a way that appeals to the child's perspective.

Teachable Moment #1: A Lie

Catalyst: You catch your child lying, or a lying scenario is presented through the media.

Truth #1: Satan is referred to as the "father of lies," and God cannot lie. Honesty comes from a redeemed heart; lying is wrong. (Exodus 20:16; Proverbs 19:22; John 8:44; Colossians 3:9; Titus 1:2)

Questions: What's the worst lie ever? (There is no God; second is that Jesus was not resurrected.) Why do you think most people lie? Has someone ever lied to you? How did you feel when that happened? How can being silent be a lie? Even if you don't get caught, who knows that you lie?

Truth #2: Lying ruins a person's credibility. He or she can't be trusted or given privileges. (Galatians 6:7)

Questions: If you lie about a little thing, will it be easier down the road to lie about a big thing? If you were I, would you trust you again? Why? How long should it take before I can trust you again? Has someone ever lied to you? How did it feel?

Teachable Moment #2: Gossip

Catalyst: Your child repeats an ugly rumor about someone.

Relationship Truth: Gossip destroys relationships and is not dignified. (1 Timothy 3:11; Proverbs 20:19; James 3:11)

Questions: How do you think so-and-so would feel if he or she heard you say that? Did you see this firsthand? If not, how do you know it's true? Even if it is true, what good will come of your telling it? Have you repeated this rumor to anyone else? What can you do to help stop rumors like that?

Teachable Moment #3: Teen Pregnancy

Catalyst: An unmarried teen that you know had sex and is pregnant.

Truth #1: Sex is intended to be enjoyed in the context of marriage; anything else is impure. (Hebrews 13:4; 1 John 2:14-16)

Questions: Why do you think God wants humans to have sex only with their marriage partners? Do you think the girl expected to get pregnant? Why do you think she decided not to wait for marriage? Is that a good reason? (Or is that what love is?) What benefits are there in being abstinent before marriage? Does abstinence make sense to you?

Truth #2: Although it is legal in this country, abortion is not a biblical option. (Psalm 139:13-16; Deuteronomy 5:17)

Questions: Under what circumstances should she consider abortion? What is best for the baby now? What are your plans for raising children?

Teachable Moment #4: Too Much on Your Plate

Catalyst: You are at an all-you-can-eat restaurant. Your child doesn't eat all the food he or she selected, or he or she chooses several desserts.

Truth: Even though the food is "free," it is still wrong to be a glutton. Self-control is a virtue. Discuss the sayings "Your eyes are bigger than your stomach" and "Eat to live; don't live to eat." (Proverbs 23:19-21; Titus 1:7-8; Galatians 5:23)

Questions: How much food is too much? What signals does your body give when it's time to stop eating? Do you listen to those signals? Who pays for the food when you don't eat it? Do you think that is taking advantage of the system? Do you think it is considerate? Do you think Jesus would do it?

Teachable Moment #5: Intoxication

Catalyst: Your child comes in contact with someone who is intoxicated.

Truth: Alcohol affects a person's body so that he or she is no longer in control of his or her actions. This is disgraceful in the eyes of God and oftentimes is hurtful to others, not to mention dangerous, especially if the intoxicated person is driving. (Proverbs 20:1; Galatians 5:19-21)

Questions: What does the Bible say about drinking alcohol? About getting drunk? Do any of your friends drink alcohol? Do you respect the actions of so-and-so now that you've seen him or her drunk? Why do you think so-and-so drinks? What will you do when you are someplace and are offered a drink? Many of your friends will start drinking. What do you plan to do if they start drinking and you're around?

Teachable Moment #6: Taking the Lord's Name in Vain

Catalyst: You are watching a movie or a TV show and someone uses the Lord's name in vain or uses foul language.

Truth #1: God does not want His name to be used in any way that is not reverent and uplifting, honoring and respectful. (Deuteronomy 5:11)

Truth #2: God also expects us to refrain from using language that does not build up or is offensive. (Ephesians 4:29, 5:4)

Questions for both truths: What are your standards for language in a movie? Under what circumstances would you turn off the TV or walk out of a movie theater? What do you think God's standards are? Do you need to re-evaluate your personal standards? Does it matter if the "bad guys" or the "good guys" use the bad language? Why or why not?

Teachable Moment #7: Feeling Ugly

Catalyst: Your child is upset about acne, a bad hair day, or is feeling fat or unmanly. He or she lets this outward "disaster" stop him or her from enjoying the day.

Truth: God does not evaluate people by their outward appearance; your child needs to learn that he or she is still valuable and still has a purpose for the day even though he or she may feel worthless. (1 Samuel 16:7; Psalm 32:10-11; Colossians 3:23-24)

Questions: Let your child know that you had days like that and still do but that you go on and help the family or go to work, etc. Will God judge you by what you look like? Even if you were the ugliest person on the earth, which you're not, can you still please God? Do your friends judge you the same way God does? Who is easier to please—God or your friends? Whom can you trust to love you no matter what you look like?

Teachable Moment #8: Pride

Catalyst: Your child participates in a sporting event, academic competition, or a game like Monopoly. He or she is successful and then makes a disparaging comment about his or her opponents.

Truth #1: It is dishonorable to bad-mouth or wish ill on your opponents or enemies. (Proverbs 17:5, 24:17-18; Romans 12:16-18)

Questions: I thought you won the game—why the nasty words? What would Jesus say about so-and-so? You are the winner, what would a good sport do? What does so-and-so feel right now? Have you ever felt that way?

Truth #2: God hates pride. (Proverbs 8:13, 11:2, 13:10, 16:18, 29:23)

Questions: What will so-and-so say about *you*? Why does winning a game or contest make you better? Who gave you that talent in the first place? Do you think God likes your attitude? Why or why not? What does God want you to do with your talents?

Teachable Moment #9: Finders Keepers

Catalyst: Your child finds something valuable in a parking lot, for example, a necklace, expensive sunglasses, or money.

Truth: Finding something that doesn't belong to you isn't stealing, but you should make every effort to find the owner. The more valuable the object is, the more effort you should put into locating the owner. It's never okay just to say, "Finders keepers, losers weepers." (Deuteronomy 22:1-3; Philippians 2:4)

Questions: Have you ever lost something and had it returned? How did that feel? Do you remember when we lost the ____?

Wouldn't it have been great if someone had returned it? When you find the owner, what will be his or her reaction? If you were a millionaire, would you still want to keep this object? Why or why not? If you really "needed" this object, wouldn't God provide for you in a way that didn't harm someone else?

Teachable Moment #10: Feeling Like a Failure

Catalyst: Your child feels like a failure; he or she has lost a competition, earned poor grades, been rejected by friends, been cut from a sports team, messed up in a piano recital, or did not find a date for the prom.

Truth: God loves him or her no matter what! Jesus died for your child before he or she was worthy. (Romans 5:6-11; 2 Corinthians 12:9-10; Hebrews 11:13)

Questions: *None.* Tell your child about a time when you felt like a failure. Let your child know that you love him or her and respect the time it will take to emotionally recover from such a big disappointment.

Teachable Moment #11: Lost!

Catalyst: Your child is lost or separated from you for a time at the mall, amusement park, or other crowded place. When you are reunited, there is a special closeness.

Truth: God feels a similar joy when your child first believes in Christ or your child repents from his or her sins. (Luke 15:3-32)

Questions: How did you feel when we were separated? Do you think I was worried? How does God feel when we are "lost" from Him when we do things that are wrong? How does God feel when we come back to Him?

Teachable Moment #12: A Scalding Scolding

Catalyst: You reprimand your child in public and then feel bad about it. You apologize. Or one of your children gets on a sibling's case in public. You ask the aggressor to apologize.

Truth: It is better to discipline someone in private; a person is more likely to receive the advice if it is done kindly and without public humiliation or embarrassment. (Matthew 18:15; Galatians 6:1)

Questions: How does it feel when someone points out your flaws in public? If someone wants you to change, what's the best way to go about letting you know? Can you think of a time when someone told you that were doing something wrong and you got angry?

Teachable Moment #13: Boasting

Catalyst: Your child thinks he or she is hot stuff because of some worldly ability, popularity, or spiritual gift.

Truth #1: We are all sinners, saved by grace. No one has anything to boast about except that God gave him gifts. (Romans 3:23, 12:3, 16-18; Galatians 5:26, 6:3)

Truth #2: To whom more is given, more is expected. God gives spiritual gifts to build up the church. All gifts should be considered as a tool to help others. (Matthew 25:14-40; Luke 17:47-48; 1 Corinthians 14:12)

Questions: Who gave you the talents you have? What do you think God wants you to do with such a great talent? Why do you think God has given you so much? Does He expect more from you, or less, because of your abilities?

Teachable Moment #14: Grumbling

Catalyst: An unpleasant task awaits your child; he or she grumbles, grumbles, grumbles.

Truth: Your child needs to learn to rise above the drudgery of certain tasks and see beyond the inconvenience and unpleasantness of work. All work is noble if done for the right reasons. Strong character and perseverance can be built in no other way. (Ecclesiastes 2:24; Philippians 2:12-18; Colossians 3:17, 23-24; James 1:2-4; Romans 5:3-5)

Questions: Do you like being around grumblers? Would you like to be around me if I complained about driving you to school, washing the dishes, going to work? Does grumbling energize you? Does it make the job easier? What's the best way to tackle a difficult job? Can you think of a time when there was something unpleasant to do, and it went by quickly because you thought about something else? What can you think of while you're doing this job? How would Jesus tackle this job?

Teachable Moment #15: A Stolen Moment

Catalyst: Your child steals something from you, a store, or a friend. Or someone your child knows has something taken from your home, yard, or your child's desk at school.

Truth #1: Respecting property rights is a key theme in the Pentateuch—don't steal! The New Testament echoes it too. (Exodus 20:15; Ephesians 4:28)

Questions: Why do you think God included "Do not steal" as one of the commandments? Do you like it when others steal from you?

Truth #2: The Lord will provide for your child; your child should learn to pray for God to supply his or her needs and pray for a way to earn money so that he or she is not tempted to steal. (Proverbs 30:7-9; Matthew 6:8-13; Ephesians 4:28; Philippians 4:19)

Questions: Is there a difference between stealing bread to eat and stealing a DVD? Why? Does God know when we need something? How? If you trust God, should it be difficult to wait for things you really want?

Teachable Moment #16: Homosexuality

Catalyst: Your child meets a person who is gay—a relative, classmate, teacher, neighbor, or friend. Or someone in the media admits to being a homosexual and has a "lifelong partner."

Truth #1: Same-sex liaisons are described as "an abomination," "shameful," "unnatural," "unrighteous," and "contrary to sound teaching." (Leviticus 18:22; Romans 1:26-32; 1 Corinthians 6:9-11; 1 Timothy 1:10)

Questions: What do you know about homosexuality? Do you know what the Bible says about it?

Truth #2: Marriage is designated in the Bible for a man and a woman. There are no biblical marriages between people of the same sex. (Genesis 2:18-25; Mark 10:6-9)

Questions: What does the Bible say about marriage? Does it make sense? Do you think gay sex partners should be allowed to get married if it's only a legal ceremony? Why or why not?

Truth #3: A non-Christian homosexual, like any non-Christian, should be won over by prayer and charity as well as be treated with respect. (1 Corinthians 5:9-12) Note: Being respectful does not mean taking safety risks.

Questions: If Jesus cared about prostitutes and tax collectors, how do you think he would treat gay people? Is it difficult for you to be around gay people? What are some of the things about homosexuality that bother you? Would those things cause you to hate or disrespect a gay person?

Truth #4: A professing Christian who struggles with homosexual desires should live a life of chastity and purity, refraining from sexual immorality. (Dr. Dobson recommends seeking professional counseling. It is probably not just a "phase," and a teen in this situation needs lots of loving support and clear teaching about the nature of human sexuality.) The same standards of self-control exist for unmarried heterosexual men and women. (1 Corinthians 6:9-11, 10:8; Titus 2:5-6)

Questions: Do you think it's possible for a person with homosexual desires to lead a life that pleases God?

Teachable Moment #17: Food for Thought

Catalyst: You or your child hears or reads about the life-preserving virtue of a food, or you are exposed to the five-a-day vegetable and fruit plan for a healthy diet.

Truth: The natural food God designed for us is nourishing; when choosing food, try to stay as close as possible to God's original packaging (fruits, vegetables, and simple grains like oatmeal). God also intends for us to eat meat. (Genesis 1:29, 9:3; Daniel 1:11-16)

Questions: How do you choose the foods you eat? Are there better choices you could be making? What foods were originally designed for humans to eat?

Teachable Moment #18: Divorce

Catalyst: Your child finds out about a marriage that is dissolving or sees a TV program or movie that presents divorce as an attractive option to people who "fell out of love" or "just couldn't get along."

Truth #1: God hates divorce; divorce is the result of hardened hearts or sexual impurity. (Malachi 2:16; 1 Corinthians 7:10-11; Mark 10:1-11)

Questions: What is a hard heart? Do people's hearts harden in an instant, or does it happen over time? Why do you think God hates divorce? Do you have a hard heart toward anyone? What can you do about it?

Truth #2: To prepare for a godly marriage, your child needs to learn respect, forgiveness, self-control (sexual purity), and self-sacrifice. (Ephesians 5:21-32; 1 Peter 3:1-7; Colossians 3:5, 12-14, 18-19)

Questions: Do you want your own marriage to last a lifetime? What kind of a husband or wife do you want to be? How can you prepare today to be a good spouse in the future? What can you do today to keep sexually pure? What are the spiritual qualities you want in a spouse? How will you recognize those?

Teachable Moment #19: Racial Slurs

Catalyst: You are with your child and hear a racially demeaning joke or remark.

Truth #1: God created all people in His image. (Genesis 1:27)

Questions: Do you think God made one group of people superior to another? Are all people created in God's image? Do you think whites/African Americans/Latin Americans/Asians, etc. were created without God's handiwork? Is God's fingerprint on every race? Do you think you should be looking for ways to despise God's creation?

Truth #2: A Christian's speech should build up other people, not tear them down. (Ephesians 4:29)

Questions: Would Jesus repeat that joke? Why or why not? What's difficult for you to understand about white/African American/Latin American/Asian, etc. people? Do those difficulties keep you from being friendly or respecting them?

Teachable Moment #20: Disrespect

Catalyst: Your child rolls his or her eyes at you, responds with sarcasm, or shows in any one of a thousand ways that he or she does not respect you.

Truth: Honoring your parents pleases the Lord. If you can't honor your parents, you will have trouble honoring a boss, a spouse, or even God. Showing respect to your parents proves you have self-control and humility. Honoring your parents trains you for success in your future. Honoring your parents keeps you from being grounded! (Deuteronomy 5:16; Ephesians 6:1)

Questions: When is someone an adult? Should adults ever stop honoring their parents? When you are a parent, are you going to let your children dishonor you? Why or why not? Why do you think God gave kids parents? How do you think parents feel when their children act disrespectfully? Why would a parent give a privilege to a disrespectful child? If a person shows disrespect to his or her parents, will it be easier or harder to respect the Lord?

Teachable Moment #21: Your Child Shares!

Catalyst: Your child makes a sacrifice to share a toy, money, or a prized possession. This is above and beyond the call of duty.

Truth: God loves a cheerful giver; affirm that your child is exhibiting a fruit of the Spirit: goodness. (Proverbs 22:9; 2 Corinthians 9:7; Galatians 5:22; 1 Timothy 6:18)

Questions: Why do you think God loves a cheerful giver? How do you feel inside? Is it the same kind of happy when you receive something? How are the feelings different? Which one is more important?

Teachable Moment #22: Kindness

Catalyst: You catch your child being kind to a sibling or neighbor when ordinarily there is strife.

Truth: Kindness is a virtue God approves of. It is a fruit of the Spirit. (Micah 6:8; Galatians 5:22; Colossians 3:12)

Questions: How did being kind make you feel? If you always treated your brother/sister like that, would our home be more like heaven? Tell me about someone who has been kind to you.

Teachable Moment #23: Repentance

Catalyst: Your child feels bad inside about something he or she did.

Truth: Repentance is good; it lets you know when you need to ask forgiveness and make amends. God is happy when people repent. (Luke 13:3, 15:8-10; 2 Corinthians 7:10)

Questions: What did you do that made you feel so bad? What do you want to do about that bad feeling? Do you know that God will forgive you for doing wrong? Do you want to ask God to forgive you? (Tell your child about something you did wrong, felt sorry for later, and asked God and others to forgive you of.)

Teachable Moment #24: Prudence

Catalyst: You see your child pushing the envelope in some area. He or she is taking risks or not planning ahead; he or she is expecting, unwisely, that things will work out. This could be not using a helmet when riding a bike, hanging around a rebellious crowd, getting sexually close to a girlfriend or boyfriend, or not studying for an important exam.

Truth: Foolishly taking risks by not planning ahead is unwise, as is seeing how close you can come to physical or spiritual danger. (Proverbs 22:3; Matthew 25:1-13, NASB)

Questions: In general, aim these questions toward getting kids to admit they don't think it will happen to them. Why couldn't it happen to you? What chances are you willing to take with sin? (Tell your child about a time you did something rash and regretted it.)

Teachable Moment #25: Diligence

Catalyst: You are helping your child with his or her homework. You notice he or she is trying to do the absolute least amount of work to comply with the assignment. Or when practicing a musical instrument or doing chores, he or she is trying to do the least amount of work to be "finished" rather than striving for quality.

Truth: Diligence in homework/chores/practice will lead to a more fruitful life. It is also a model for being spiritually diligent. (Proverbs 10:4, 21:5; 2 Timothy 2:15, NASB)

Questions: Why are you trying to do the least amount of work? If you were the teacher, how would you grade this? Do you think God knows when you are diligently trying to be His good servant and when you are you just trying to get by? Even if you get an A on that assignment, how would God grade you? What kind of habits do you want to develop when it comes to homework and spiritual work?

Teachable Moment #26: Scheming

Catalyst: Your child is caught scheming in some way: trying to get out of doing chores, get more allowance, take privileges from siblings, finagle a later curfew; use half-truths to avoid work.

Truth: Dishonesty does not produce spiritual fruit. (Proverbs 24:8-9; Philippians 2:4)

Questions: Are you putting all this energy into pleasing yourself or pleasing God? Would Jesus use that argument? Who are you worried about, you or the other person? What will the people you schemed against think when they find out you're a Christian?

Teachable Moment #27: Selfishness

Catalyst: Your child badgers you to buy something, and you've already said no.

Truth: A selfish person's appetite is never satisfied. Only God can truly satisfy. (Psalm 73: 25; Proverbs 27:20; Ecclesiastes 5:10, 6:7)

Questions: How long will you treasure this? What will you want next week? What will you want next year? How can you earn the money to buy that? What is the one thing that you can desire and always have more than enough of? (Tell about a time when you desired something, but once you possessed it, the object didn't give you the satisfaction you had hoped for.)

Teachable Moment #28: Violence on TV

Catalyst: A movie or TV program is grossly violent.

Truth: Violence does not please God; it won't be part of heaven; it should not be part of our thoughts. (Psalm 11:5; Proverbs 3:31; Isaiah 60:18; Philippians 4:8)

Questions: What appeals to you about this movie? Would you really want to see that in real life? When would you turn off the TV—how much violence is too much? Should you be trying to see how close you can come to that standard before turning off the TV, or should you strive to keep away from that line?

Teachable Moment #29: God Created You

Catalyst: Your child expresses awe at seeing a newborn or a documentary about the complexities of the human body.

Truth: God is the Creator; He carefully crafted everything about you. (Genesis 1:27; Psalm 100:3, 139:13-16)

Questions: What do you feel when you see a little baby's fingers and toes? Can words even describe the awesome intricacies of the human body? Do you think God still cares for people He created? Why or why not?

Teachable Moment #30: Choice Words

Catalyst: Your child says something that is hurtful, even if it is true.

Truth: Staying silent is better than using hurtful words. (Proverbs 17:28; Ecclesiastes 3:1,7; Matthew 12:36; Ephesians 4:32)

Questions: How do you think so-and-so felt when you said that? Does so-and-so think you are kind? If so-and-so wanted to become a Christian, would he or she ask you about God? Can you tell me about a time when someone said something mean to you? How did you feel? How does God want us to talk to one another?

Teachable Moment #31: Sleepy Head

Catalyst: Your child does not want to go to church because he or she went to bed too late on Saturday.

Truth: The church needs your child, and he or she should plan ahead to worship. (Hebrews 10:25; 1 Corinthians 12:27)

Questions: What things *should be* more important than meeting with other Christians? What things *actually are* more important to you than church? What would you like to do at church that would make it more meaningful to you? Do you go to give, to get, or both? What gifts do you have to offer the church?

Teachable Moment #32: Vengeance

Catalyst: Your child gets angry and hurts someone physically or emotionally. Or the media portrays someone who wants to take revenge.

Truth #1: Anger does not accomplish what God desires. (Proverbs 29:22; Ephesians 4:26; James 1:19-20)

Questions: When you were angry, were you in control, or was the anger? Do you feel better? How does so-and-so feel? Is that what God wants? What can you do to be in control next time?

Truth #2: Retribution or "pay back" is God's job. (Deuteronomy 32:35; Romans 12:21)

Questions: According to the Bible, is there any reason to justify doing something mean to another person? Did you really want so-and-so hurt? Has someone done that to you? How does it feel?

Teachable Moment #33: Rash Words

Catalyst: Your child says something rash like "I hate you!" "He's a complete idiot!" or "I wish she'd never been born!"

Truth: We will be held accountable for the words we speak. (Proverbs 12:23, 18:7; Matthew 5:21-22; James 3:1-12, 5:9)

Questions: Do you really mean that? How are words crueler sometimes than physical blows? Tell me what "Sticks and stones may break my bones but words will never hurt me" means. Is it true? If I said that about you, how would you feel? (Tell your child about something mean someone said to you and how it affected you.)

Teachable Moment #34: Birthday Party Planning

Catalyst: A birthday party or other celebration is being planned.

Truth #1: God has plans for your child's life; He is interested in your child's future and wants your child to anticipate it with joy. (Jeremiah 29:11)

Truth #2: Your child needs to be seeking God through prayer and with his or her whole heart to appreciate this plan. (Jeremiah 29:12-13)

Questions: This is a nice party you're planning—do you think God has plans for you this year? How can you find out what those plans are? What are the things that could stop you from enjoying a future with Him? What would His invitation offer? Would you accept that invitation?

Teachable Moment #35: Crash!

Catalyst: You pass by a car crash site with rescue workers attending to a victim or victims.

Truth #1: God heals our wounds. (Jeremiah 33:6; James 5:15-16)

Questions: None. Pray for the victim, the victim's family, and for the rescue workers.

Truth #2: No one knows the hour at which he will die or when tragedy will strike. (Ecclesiastes 9:12; Luke 12:16-21; 1 Thessalonians 5:12)

Questions: What do you think the driver of that car was thinking this morning? Do you think he was prepared for this event? If you died today, would you be ready? What does the Bible say about being ready for when Jesus comes?

Teachable Moment #36: Saturn Is Rising

Catalyst: You see the Zodiac symbols or a horoscope forecast.

Truth #1: The stars and planets move at God's command. The heavens are evidence that He is the mighty Creator. (Genesis 1:1; Nehemiah 9:6; Psalm 8:3, 19:1, 97:6, 102:25; Romans 1:20)

Questions: Who made the heavens and the earth? What is the message the stars give us? Why seek answers from the stars when we can ask God, their Creator, directly through prayer?

Truth #2: Trying to predict the future or derive personality traits from the stars and planets is divination. God is the source of wisdom. We should seek Him and not get tangled up in witchcraft or fortune-telling. (Leviticus 19:26; 2 Kings 17:16-17, 21:6; Galatians 5:19-20)

Questions: Who knows the future? What good is it seeking messages from the stars? Is it harmless, or do people who read horoscopes displease God? How can you obtain wisdom? Why do you think people seek information from the stars or crystal balls and the like? Where do you seek knowledge and wisdom? If you trust God for your future, does it matter what the future is?

Teachable Moment #37: A Suit of Armor

Catalyst: You see a suit of armor, a sword, or a picture of a knight or Roman soldier.

Truth: Faith is like a suit of armor to protect us from evil powers. (Belt of truth, breastplate of righteousness, shield of faith—Ephesians 6:10-18)

Questions: How do you plan on protecting yourself against Satan or temptation? How can you keep your mind from accepting false information—attacks on your thinking? How can you prepare for spiritual battle? What happens if you're not prepared?

Teachable Moment #38: Rules

Catalyst: You are playing a board game and must consult the rules.

Truth: The Bible is our rule book for life. By following it, we can find out how to receive eternal life. (Psalm 119:105; Proverbs 6:23; Proverbs 3:5-6)

Questions: What happens when you follow the Bible's rules? What happens when you don't? Does everyone believe the Bible is the rule book for life? Do you? What parts of the Bible are the most difficult for you to follow? (Tell your child about an instance when you followed the Bible because you knew it was the right way, not because it was easy.)

Teachable Moment #39: Hand Washing

Catalyst: You and your child are washing your hands together.

Truth: Just as washing with soap makes your hands clean, so the

Bible, or Word of God, cleanses the soul or heart of a person. (John 15:3; Ephesians 5:26)

Questions: What can purify a person's heart? Why does a heart need to be cleansed? Can you think of a time when your heart was cleansed? How is washing your hands similar? If you wash your hands once, is that enough to keep you clean and healthy? If you cleanse your heart once, is that enough to keep you walking in purity and integrity? (Now would be a good time to share a time when the Bible's teaching made you have a change of heart.)

Teachable Moment #40: The Seasons Change

Catalyst: The first frost of winter comes, the trees' leaves change colors, the days begin to lengthen for summer, or the crocuses bloom.

Truth: Just as the seasons are on a schedule, so is the Lord. He will return. Be ready. (Matthew 24:7; Philippians 4:5; James 5:7)

Questions: Jesus said He is coming back; do you believe it? If Jesus were coming back tomorrow, what would you do today? How can you become ready?

Teachable Moment #41: Prayer

Catalyst: You pray with your child.

Truth: The Lord wants us to pray for His will to be done on this earth, for our physical needs, for forgiveness, and for strength to resist evil. (Matthew 6:9-15)

Questions: Why does God want us to pray for forgiveness? What is God's will, and how can we know it? If we pray to win the lottery, will God answer that prayer? Why or why not? Do you pray daily for strength to resist temptation and to fight your sin nature?

Teachable Moment #42: Old People

Catalyst: The media caricatures someone old as grumpy, ugly, foolish, or otherwise undesirable.

Truth: God wants us to honor our elders because they are wise. Forty-two youths who made fun of the prophet Elisha's baldness were attacked by bears because of their disrespect. Do not mock your elders. (Exodus 20:12; 2 Kings 2:23-24; Proverbs 3:35 NASB, 16:31, 20:29; 1 Peter 5:5)

Questions: Why doesn't our culture honor old people? What is weakness in God's eyes? Are old people weak? Can you tell me about an older person whom you respect? What do you want to be like when you are old? What are your plans for becoming the type of old person that people respect?

Teachable Moment #43: Overweight People

Catalyst: A joke about an overweight person is made on TV or within your child's hearing. Or your child makes a rude comment about someone's weight.

Truth #1: God looks at a person's heart, not his or her appearance. (1 Samuel 16:7)

Questions: If so-and-so heard that remark, how would he or she feel? Does God see so-and-so differently than you do? Whose opinion is the most valid? How do you want to be judged? Would Jesus have said that? Sure, many overweight people are also overeaters, but just because their sin is visible, does that mean that they are not forgiven or trying to do what's right? What kinds of sins do people commit that you can't see the results? Why is it popular to make fun of overweight people?

Truth #2: Proverbs 6:17 says that God hates "haughty eyes."

Questions: The Bible says that God hates haughty eyes, or prideful people. Fat people aren't on the list; which is worse in God's eyes—to be fat or to make fun of people who are fat?

Teachable Moment #44: **Teenagers**

Catalyst: You hear something in the media about teen problems or rebellion.

Truth: The Bible does not distinguish teenagers as separate from children or adults. You are not supposed to let people look down on you because you are young. Older teens are held to the same standards as adults. (1 Timothy 4:12; Titus 2:6)

Questions: Why do you think the world looks at teens as a separate category from children or adults? Why do courts try older teens as adults when they do something grossly violent? Does the Bible have lower standards of conduct for teens than for adults? Why or why not?

Teachable Moment #45: Warehouse

Catalyst: You are in a large warehouse-type store and are overwhelmed by all the merchandise.

Truth: God is your provider and has the wealth of the universe at His disposal. (Leviticus 26:5; Deuteronomy 30:9; Psalm 132:15; Isaiah 30:23; Matthew 6:28-34)

Questions: Do you ever doubt that God can provide for you? Do you trust that God will provide everything you need? Why or why not?

Teachable Moment #46: Wickedness Does Not Rest

Catalyst: You read in the newspaper about someone who has committed multiple crimes.

Truth: Evil people do not rest; evil is a pattern the wicked seek with zeal. (Proverbs 1:16, 4:16, 6:18; Isaiah 59:7; Romans 3:15)

Questions: Why is evil described as a habit? What is the only thing that can break that bad streak? The Scriptures tell us not to associate with evil people. Why?

Teachable Moment #47: Busybodies

Catalyst: Someone is sticking his or her nose into someone else's business.

Truth: God does not want us concerned with people and issues that are not in our circle of responsibility. (1 Timothy 5:13; 1 Peter 4:15)

Questions: If people have time to be involved in things that don't concern them, what should they be doing instead? Why is being a meddler displeasing to God? Do you like it when outsiders give you advice about something they don't understand? Why would that cause problems? What can you do to keep from being a busybody?

Teachable Moment #48: Military Uniform

Catalyst: You see someone in a military uniform.

Truth #1: Christians are called to fight a spiritual battle of faith. (1 Timothy 1:18-19, 6:12)

Questions: Are we enlisted in God's army? In what way? Who is our ultimate boss? Why is it called a fight?

Truth #2: Good soldiers for Christ don't get caught up in civilian affairs. (2 Titus 2:4)

Questions: Why aren't Christians supposed to cling to worldly things or values? What things keep you from serving God?

Teachable Moment #49: Beauty Can Be Deceitful

Catalyst: Someone outside your family is praised for his outward beauty.

Truth: Outward beauty is not indicative of inward beauty; often, being beautiful or handsome is a stumbling block. For example, Absalom, one of David's sons, was handsome, but he also murdered his brother and tried to steal his father's throne by force. (1 Samuel 16:7; 2 Samuel 13:28-29, 14:25, 15:13-14, 18:9; Proverbs 31:30)

Questions: Why do you think people in general are attracted to people who are good looking? How much time do you spend trying to look good? Who are you trying to please with your good looks? Is looking good a godly goal? How do you choose your friends or dates?

Teachable Moment #50: Scary Movies

Catalyst: You see an ad for a frightening movie, or your kids begin to watch one.

Truth: You are supposed to let your mind dwell on good things, not evil things. (1 Samuel 12: 24; Philippians 4:8)

Questions: Would Jesus watch that movie? Why or why not? Do you think those images from that movie are wholesome? How long will it be before the bad thoughts or images disappear? Do you want to pray so that Jesus will take away those bad pictures in your mind?

Teachable Moment #51: Roadblock

Catalyst: You come to a dead end, a train, a traffic jam, or some other obstacle in the road.

Truth: Sometimes sin blocks prayer, specifically unforgiveness, disobedience, secret sin, self-indulgence, or treating a wife with disrespect. (Deuteronomy 1:45; Psalm 66:18; Matthew 6:15; James 4:3; 1 Peter 3:7)

Questions: Why does God require us to forgive our enemies? Why wouldn't God answer a request for lots of money? Why is it important for our sins to be confessed before God will listen to us? Can you describe in relationship terms what happens when prayer is blocked? Why would God not listen to the prayers of a man who treats his wife disrespectfully? What can you do to repair your relationship with God?

Teachable Moment #52: Butterfly Lessons

Catalyst: A butterfly flutters by.

Truth: Just as a butterfly transforms into a new creation, Jesus makes us completely new. (2 Corinthians 5:17)

Questions: Are you new-and-improved like a laundry liquid with added stain-fighting crystals, or are you a completely different product once you accept Christ? In what ways are you different? Why do you suppose it sometimes feels as if you are the same old person? If a non-Christian is a good, moral person, is that the same as being a new creation? Why or why not?

Teachable Moment #53: Kite String

Catalyst: You see a kite flying high.

Truth: Obedience keeps us connected to God and allows us to be in His will. Even Jesus had to obey. (2 Chronicles 31:20; Isaiah 1:19; Hebrews 5:8-9)

Questions: Make sure your children understand that kites fly because of the wind *and* the string. Ask them what happens when a kite's string is cut. (It falls.) Our obedience is like the string that keeps us connected to God; the wind is like the Holy Spirit (John 3:8). Kites look as if they are soaring on their own, but it is the string that keeps them up. If we stay connected to God through obedience, what will happen? If we disobey God, what will happen?

Teachable Moment #54: A Rainbow Reminder

Catalyst: You see a rainbow.

Truth: God keeps His promises. The rainbow is God's symbol that He has promised never to flood the whole earth again. (Genesis 9:8-17; Deuteronomy 7:9; 1 Kings 8:56; 1 Peter 4:19).

Questions: How long has God kept His promise not to flood the entire earth? Does He keep all of His promises? If He is faithful, why is it sometimes difficult to trust Him? What can we focus on when we doubt? What promises has He kept for you? (Talk with your child about a time when God was faithful to you.)

Teachable Moment #55: The "Three Little Pigs"

Catalyst: You tell or read the story of the "Three Little Pigs" to your child.

Truth: The "Three Little Pigs" story is a lot like the parable of the man who built his house on the rock. We are to build our spiritual houses carefully so that they can withstand the trials of life. (Matthew 7:24-27)

Questions: What are we to base our faith, our spiritual houses, on? What happens when the wind (or the wolf) blows against the house that wasn't built on Jesus' teaching? Who built his house the wrong way? What are some good things we can do to make sure our houses are strong?

Teachable Moment #56: Sweet Symbol

Catalyst: Your child receives a candy cane.

Truth #1: The candy cane is shaped like a shepherd's crook and represents that Jesus is the Good Shepherd. (Psalm 23; John 10:11)

Questions: In what way are Christians like sheep? What does a shepherd do? If a sheep leaves the flock, what does a good shepherd do? (Talk about a time when Jesus led you through a troubling time.)

Truth #2: The candy cane is also shaped like a *J* for Jesus. At His name, every knee should bow. (Philippians 2:10)

Questions: In what way is Jesus' name different and powerful? Why does the Bible warn against taking the names of God in vain?

Truth #3: The red stripes represent Jesus' blood, which was shed for the forgiveness of sins. (Romans 3:25, 5:9; Hebrews 9:14)

Questions: Why is the blood so important? Does this make sense to you? Why or why not?

Truth #4: The white stripes represent Jesus' purity and holy life without sin or stain. (James 3:17; Hebrews 9:14; 1 Peter 1:19, 2:22)

Questions: If Jesus wasn't sinless, would that make a difference? Why or why not? Do you believe that Jesus was without sin? How does God perceive you? Are you seen as sinless too? Why or why not?

Teachable Moment #57: A Twisted Pretzel

Catalyst: Your family is sitting around munching on the round type pretzels with the cross in the middle.

Truth: Background—The word *pretzel* comes from the Latin *bracellus,* meaning *bracelet.* One tradition says the original circular pretzels came to be made with a cross in the middle, to be used as treats to give children for saying prayers. Everyone needs prayer, and through it we are blessed. (Psalm 65:2, 91:15; Isaiah 56:7; Luke 11:9)

Questions: Why is prayer important? Why do we need to pray? What do you feel like when you don't pray? How does God honor prayer? Do you want to pray more? What is your plan for praying more often?

Teachable Moment #58: The Sun

Catalyst: You observe with your child the sun's radiance.

Truth: A Christian's life is supposed to shine like the radiant sun. (Job 11:17; Psalm 34:5; Ecclesiastes 8:1; Daniel 12:3; John 5:35; Acts 6:15; 2 Corinthians 3:18)

Questions: Can you think of a person whose life shines brightly? Can you think of someone who is beautiful because of the presence of Christ in his or her life? What would it take for your life to shine brighter? What is your plan?

Teachable Moment #59: A Flashlight

Catalyst: You are on a camping trip or your house experiences a power failure. You need to use a flashlight to light your way.

Truth: God's Word lights our path when we can't see ahead. But it doesn't show us our entire future, just where our next few steps should be. (Psalm 119:105)

Questions: Why is it difficult sometimes to follow God's path? Why would you be tempted to leave it? How can you be sure you are staying on God's path?

Teachable Moment #60: Vines

Catalyst: You note some grape or other lush, fruit-bearing vines.

Truth: Jesus is the vine and we are the branches. (John 15:1-8)

Questions: What is the fruit in your life? Can you bear fruit apart from God? When you bear fruit, who should get the credit?

Teachable Moment #61: The Bare Facts

Catalyst: Your child sees a billboard, magazine cover, or media presentation of a provocative woman or man.

Truth #1: Christians, especially women, are supposed to dress modestly to avoid sexually tempting someone. (Romans 14:13, 21; 1 Timothy 2:8; 1 Peter 3:3-4)

Questions: Why is publicly exhibiting the human body for sexual arousal wrong? What is modest attire by today's standards? Is that the Bible's standard? Why would someone dress (or undress) in public? Is sexual attention a healthy attention outside of marriage? What are your standards for modest clothing?

Truth #2: When you see pictures like this one or ones that are even more explicit, you should move on and forget about them as soon as possible. We are to "flee sexual immorality." (Genesis 39:1-7; 1 Corinthians 6:18; 2 Timothy 2:22)

Questions: Why should we "flee from" and not "flirt with" sexually stimulating pictures or people? Is sexual immorality something that is easy to avoid? What is your plan if you are with friends who chose to look at pornography?

Truth #3: There's a common saying in the world: "It's okay to look as long as you don't touch." This is not the biblical perspective. Jesus said even considering the act of sex outside of marriage is as good as doing it. Letting your mind dwell on lustful thoughts is wrong. (Matthew 5:27-30)

Questions: What does Jesus mean when He talks about lust? Is lust thinking, *Wow, he or she is really cute*? What are the boundaries between "lust" and "like"? How can you avoid approaching the lust line? How does a lustful person act when he or she is in a romantic relationship? How does a loving person act when he or she is in a romantic relationship? Under what circumstances during a date is lust likely to emerge? How can you avoid those?

Thirty-Five Biblical Object Lessons

1. A large tree growing by a river teaches that God takes care of those who stay away from evil and wicked people—Psalm 1; Jeremiah 17:7-8.
2. A starry night testifies that there is a Creator, an intelligent, powerful God—Psalm 19:1, 97:6; Romans 1:20.
3. The wind is an example of the Holy Spirit's working in our lives—John 3:8.
4. The way God cares for sparrows teaches us that He cares for us—Psalm 84:3; Matthew 10:29, 31.
5. An ant colony represents the virtue of diligence—Proverbs 6:6-8, 30:24-25.
6. A lion represents the devil, who is waiting to devour us if we let our guard down—1 Peter 5:8-9.
7. An eagle's strength is an example of someone who depends on the Lord—Isaiah 40:30-31.
8. The fact that babies crave milk is an example of a new Christian, hungry for pure food—1 Peter 2:2.
9. Clay represents us in the hands of God, moldable for His purposes—Isaiah 64:8; Jeremiah 18:6.
10. Honey is likened to Scriptures; honey is sweet to the tongue and Scripture is sweet to the soul—Psalm 119:103.
11. Water is used often to refer to "life" or spiritual baptism—John 4:14; Acts 10:47; Revelation 22:1.
12. Jesus called himself the "light"—John 8:12.

13. Jesus calls followers salt; kind, thoughtful speech is also compared to salt—Matthew 5:13; Colossians 4:6.
14. Jesus is the "Lamb of God"—John 1:29, 36.
15. The farm term *harvest* is used to describe people ready to convert to Christianity—Matthew 9:35-37; Luke 10:2.
16. Jesus used seeds as an example of truths and the kingdom of heaven—Matthew 13:19-23, 31-32.
17. Thorns represent worthless faith—Hebrews 6:8.
18. Fire is used to describe the way a person's words can be hurtful—James 3:5-6.
19. Fire is also used to describe the power of God's Word—Jeremiah 5:14.
20. God's yearning to keep His people safe is described as a hen gathering chicks under her wings—Luke 13:34.
21. Lizards are said to be wise because they are so small and yet live in the palaces of kings—Proverbs 30:28.
22. God's Word is food for the soul—Deuteronomy 8:3.
23. God's Word is also like a sword, piercing the soul—Hebrews 4:12.
24. A crown represents the gift of faith, proof of enduring faith—Revelation 2:17.
25. Turbulent water represents suffering or trials—Psalm 73:10, 69:1-2.
26. God is a rock, a place of refuge—Isaiah 26:4.
27. Men and women of faith are like a pillar in the temple—Revelation 3:12.
28. God is like a fortress—2 Samuel 22:2; Psalm 18:2.
29. A well and the water in it are a metaphor for salvation—Isaiah 12:3.
30. Yeast or leaven (baking powder or baking soda) is compared to sin—1 Corinthians 5:6.
31. A pig represents someone who cannot appreciate spiritual things—Proverbs 11:22; Matthew 7:6.

32. A pit is a metaphor for being in trouble or caught in sin—Psalm 7:5, 40:2, 103:4; Proverbs 23:27; Matthew 15:14.
33. A plank or a board represents blindness to your faults—Matthew 7:3; Luke 6:41.
34. Fruit is used as a metaphor to indicate spiritual maturity or prosperity—Matthew 3:8-10, 7:16-20; Galatians 5:22.
35. Flocks of sheep represent Christians—Matthew 25:32-33; John 10; 1 Peter 5:2.

Five Milestone Truths

Milestone Moment #1: Baptism

Baptism is a public ceremony at which a Christian confesses his or her faith in Jesus Christ's ability to forgive sins and provide salvation. It is an act of obedience and satisfies the older child's desire to commit to the teachings of Christ.

Catalyst: Your child expresses a desire to accept Jesus as his or her savior, or he or she wasn't baptized as an infant and wants to be now. If a child is very young, it's up to the parent to decide if baptism is appropriate, depending on whether or not the child is mature enough to understand the commitment and cost of such a decision. When baptism is the answer, set aside an hour or so to go over the truths associated with this spiritual milestone. If your child was baptized as an infant and you sense a desire in his or her heart for a forum for public confession, check into a rite of passage or blessing ceremony. (See chapter 9 for details.)

Truth #1: Jesus was baptized and we should follow His example. (Matthew 3:13-17)

Truth #2: Getting baptized answers the feeling you have that asks, "What do I do to show God I believe?" (Acts 2:14, 36-4)

Truth #3: Many people, upon becoming saved, immediately were baptized. (Acts 10, 16:11-15)

Truth #4: Baptism represents being cleansed from our sin nature and being renewed through spiritual life. It is an outward sign of inward repentance. (Romans 6:3-7; 1 Peter 3:21-22)

Questions: Tell me what you know about baptism. Why do you want to be baptized? What are good reasons to be baptized? Do you understand the symbolism surrounding baptism? How do you want to be baptized?

Milestone Moment #2: Communion

Catalyst: Your child exhibits a desire to know more about Communion; you as a parent ask questions, and your child reveals he or she is ready to delve deeper into the meaning of this mystical and wonderful sacrament.

Truth #1: The wine represents Jesus' blood, which was poured out for the forgiveness of sins. (Matthew 26:17-30)

Truth #2: The bread represents Jesus' body, which was given for the life of the world. Jesus is the living bread. (John 6:48-58)

Truth #3: When you take Communion, it is to remember what Christ did for us. (1 Corinthians 11:23-26)

Truth #4: Self-examination is part of the Christian life. You need to check your motives and confess your sins regularly. (1 Corinthians 11:27-29)

Questions: Why do Christians observe Communion? Why is taking Communion so important? What does the bread symbolize? What does the wine symbolize? Why do we keep taking Communion? Isn't once enough, as with baptism?

Milestone Moment #3: Preparing for Adolescence

Catalyst: Hormones. This is one of the times you act before the catalyst of puberty hits. The prime time for most children is between the ages of 10 and 12.

Truth #1: Adolescence is a difficult time, but you have help to avoid some of the pain and confusion. God and I will put rules in place to help and protect you and to teach you self-discipline. The result is what we're both seeking—independence for you. (Hebrews 12:11)

Questions: What do you think will be the most difficult part of growing up? As you get older, will it be easier or more difficult to obey your parents? What will you do when you want to do something and I say no? Why do you think I make rules for you to follow? Why do you think God makes rules for everyone to follow?

Truth #2: Kids need to be careful about their choice of friends. (Proverbs 13:20, 18:24)

Questions: How do you choose your friends? What are some of the qualities friends should have? (Tell your child about a friend who has helped you be a stronger Christian.)

Truth #3: The values of God and the world are different. As Christians, we are to cling to God's values and shun the world's values. (Romans 12:2; 1 Samuel 16:7)

Questions: What values do you have that are different from your non-Christian friends' values? What are God's values based on? What are the world's values based on? Which set of values is more difficult to adhere to? Why? Which set of values will produce eternal life? Which set of values will produce joy and peace in your life right now? Which of God's standards or values is the most difficult for you to understand?

Truth #4: Emotions can't be trusted to steer us in ways that will please God. (Proverbs 3:5-6; Psalm 94:17-22)

Questions: In what ways are emotions good? Which emotions make it easier to follow God's laws? Which emotions sometimes lead us astray in our thinking or self-discipline? Which emotions are the most difficult for you to control?

Truth #5: God has given you certain gifts. You need to discover what they are and how to use them. (Romans 12:4-8; 1 Corinthians 12)

Questions: What gifts do you think you have? Have you seen evidence of this? What would you like to do for God? Do you think He will equip you to do that? What is the best time you've ever had serving someone else?

Truth #6: Jesus grew physically too. Your body will change as it prepares for adulthood. (Luke 2:52)

Questions: What are you thinking about the changes that will occur in your body? How does it make you feel to know that soon you will become a man or a woman? What would you like to happen when you are an adult? Is there anything about growing up that you're concerned about?

Milestone Moment #4: Purity

Catalyst: Your child turns about 13 and has an ever-increasing interest in the opposite sex.

Truth #1: You do not own your body: Christ does. He will help keep your body holy. Keeping sexually pure by handling sexual temptation is a godly goal. Your friends might tempt you to look at pornography in magazines, movies, or on the Internet. The use of pornography is never pleasing to God. You might also be encouraged to have sexual contact, or someone might try to touch you in private places. Outside of marriage, those actions displease God. (1 Corinthians 6:13-20; Hebrews 4:14-16)

Questions: What do these verses teach about our bodies? How will Jesus help us?

Truth #2: Just because someone is a virgin doesn't make him or her sexually pure. You need to keep your mind pure as well as your body. (Matthew 5:27-30)

Questions: How are we to do this? What makes you tempted to dwell on sex? Do you have a plan for keeping your mind pure? What is it?

(See also Teachable Moments #3, #16, #18, and #61.)

Milestone Moment #5: Rite of Passage

Catalyst: When your child is crossing into adulthood, age 15 or older.

(There are a great many more truths you can cover in this milestone moment. If you need more information see *Spiritual Milestones* by J. Otis and Gail Ledbetter, and Jim and Janet Weidmann.)

Truth #1: Our greatest priority is to seek God. (Matthew 22:34-40)

Questions: Why does the Bible say that? How does this command set priorities for the rest of life? What are the things in your life that may get in the way of seeking God? Is seeking God first always convenient? What do you do when there is a price to pay for seeking God?

Truth #2: There are many things that try to grab our attention away from God. (Matthew 6:31-33)

Questions: Do you have a plan for keeping your spiritual goals top priority? What is it? How has it been working? What's the hardest thing for you to do? How will God help you? Is God more interested in relationships than in things? How do you spend your time? Is that how God wants you to spend it? (Talk about a time when you stayed focused on God and He rewarded you, or about a time when you didn't and you had to pay the consequences.)

Truth #3: You must train to live a godly life. (1 Corinthians 9:25-27)

Questions: What are you training for? In what ways does a Christian train? What ways have you trained yourself for non-spiritual pursuits? How was that similar to or different from spiritual training?

Truth #4: The Holy Spirit keeps our relationship with our heavenly Father alive; the Holy Spirit lets us know God. (1 Corinthians 2:6-16; Galatians 5:22-23)

Questions: What does this mean to you? How is this working out in your life? In what areas do you wish you knew God better?

Ten Resources for Teachable Moments Success

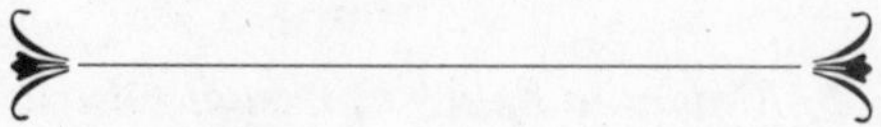

Bedtime Blessings by John Trent, Ph.D. (Wheaton, Ill.: Tyndale/Focus on the Family, 2000). Designed for use with children ages seven and under. *Bedtime Blessings* will help affirm the great love and value you and God have for your child and will help each of your evenings together be filled with cherished moments.

"Family Night Tool Chest" series by Jim Weidmann and Kurt Bruner with Mike and Amy Nappa and others (Colorado Springs, Colo.: Cook Communications, 1997–1998). *Introduction, Christian Character Qualities,* and *Basic Christian Beliefs*. Each volume offers dozens of catalysts for planned teachable moments. Your family will never forget the wild and fun lessons designed by parents like you who want learning to be exciting and accessible.

Focus on the Family Clubhouse Family Activity Book edited by Marianne Hering (Wheaton, Ill.: Tyndale/Focus on the Family, 2001). This book offers fun family activities to structure relationship time and introduce new hobbies. It also has teachable-moment helps that will allow you draw out spiritual truths from the dynamic games, crafts, recipes, and activities.

Mealtime Moments: 164 Faith-Filled Entrees to Stir Family Discussions compiled by Elaine Osborne (Wheaton, Ill.: Tyndale/Focus on the Family, 2000). *Mealtime Moments* brings you great discussion starters and activities for teaching your children about your faith. (You don't have to use them just at dinner; keep the book in your car glove box for some spur-of-the-moment teachable times.)

Movie Nights: 25 Movies to Spark Spiritual Discussions with Your Teen edited by Bob Smithouser (Wheaton, Ill.: Tyndale/Focus on the Family, 2002). *Movie Nights* converts 25 entertaining, thought-provoking films into dynamic opportunities for teachable moments. The lessons will help your teens critically evaluate the media they consume. Each chapter features discussion questions, activities, and related Scriptures.

Parents' Guide to the Spiritual Mentoring of Teens edited by Joe White and Jim Weidmann (Wheaton, Ill.: Tyndale/Focus on the Family, 2001). Learn how to walk alongside your teen as your parenting role changes from teacher to mentor. Know how to keep your parent-teen relationship rock-solid strong. Ignite in your teens the passion to be wholehearted disciples.

Parents' Guide to the Spiritual Growth of Children edited by John Trent, Ph.D., Rick Osborne, and Kurt Bruner (Wheaton, Ill.: Tyndale/Focus on the Family, 2000). This handy manual provides relationship-building tips as well as a spiritual developmental outline for children, from newborns to age 12. It will help you share the content of your teachable moments during those years when your children are most open to learning from a parent.

Raising a Modern-Day Knight by Robert Lewis (Wheaton, Ill.: Tyndale/Focus on the Family, 1997). Parents of boys who want ideas for a great relationship and a model for effective teachable moments won't want to miss this classic manual for raising godly sons.

Spiritual Milestones by Jim and Janet Weidmann and J. Otis and Gail Ledbetter (Colorado Springs, Colo.: Cook Communications, 2002). This comprehensive and practical guide for parents will help you develop a personal and intentional plan for celebrating the spiritual growth of your children. It will help you design special teachable moments that use ceremony to cement the memories.

801 Questions Kids Ask About God With Answers from the Bible compiled by Alisa Baker (Wheaton, Ill.: Tyndale/Focus on the Family, 2000). Need help finding the right truth to teach your kids? Here's a list with biblical answers that gets at the heart of what kids need—and want—to know about God.

About the Authors

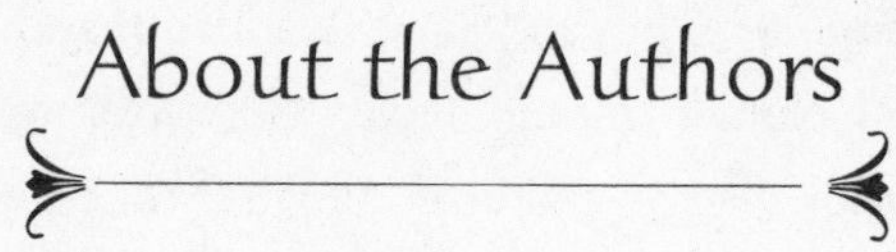

Jim Weidmann serves Focus on the Family as executive director of Heritage Builders Ministry. He also serves as vice chairman of the National Day of Prayer Task Force. He is co-author of *Family Night Tool Chest,* which shows parents how to impart biblical truths to their children in fun and imaginative ways. A former Air Force pilot, Jim has been married to his wife, Janet, for more than 20 years. They have four children.

Marianne Hering, former editor of Focus on the Family's *Clubhouse* magazine, has written hundreds of magazine articles and numerous fiction books for children. Currently she is a freelance writer living in Colorado Springs with her husband, Doug, and their three children.